TEAM UP!

The Family Ministry Playbook for
PARTNERING WITH PARENTS

PHIL BELL

Group

LOVELAND, COLORADO
group.com

Group resources really work!

This Group resource incorporates our R.E.A.L. approach to ministry. It reinforces a growing friendship with Jesus, encourages long-term learning, and results in life transformation, because it's

Relational
Learner-to-learner interaction enhances learning and builds Christian friendships.

Experiential
What learners experience through discussion and action sticks with them up to 9 times longer than what they simply hear or read.

Applicable
The aim of Christian education is to equip learners to be both hearers and doers of God's Word.

Learner-based
Learners understand and retain more when the learning process takes into consideration how they learn best.

The Family Ministry Playbook for PARTNERING WITH PARENTS

Copyright © 2015 Group Publishing, Inc.

Visit our website: **group.com**

CREDITS

Author: Phil Bell

Executive Editor: Amy Nappa

Managing Editor: Jennifer Hooks

Associate Editors: Scott Firestone IV
and Owen Shattuck

Assistant Editor: Becky Helzer

Cover Designer: Sheila Reinhardt

Book Designer: Jean Bruns

Print Production Artist: Suzi Jensen

LIBRARY OF CONGRESS CATALOGING-IN-PUBLICATION DATA

Bell, Phil, 1974-
   Team up! : the ministry playbook for partnering with parents / Phil Bell ; foreword by Jim Burns. -- First American Paperback [edition].
      pages cm
   Includes bibliographical references.
   ISBN 978-1-4707-2401-6 (pbk.)
1. Church work with youth. 2. Church work with parents. 3. Christian education of children. 4. Parenting--Religious aspects--Christianity. 5. Child rearing--Religious aspects--Christianity. I. Title.
   BV4447.B453 2015
   259'.1--dc23

                                    2015021172

ISBN: 978-1-4707-2401-6

10 9 8 7 6 5 4 3 2 1   20 19 18 17 16 15

Printed in the United States of America.

Contents

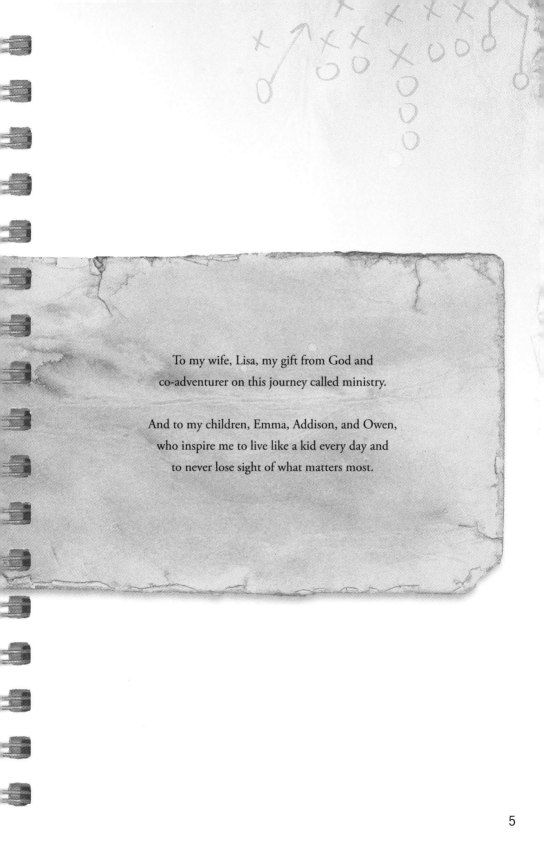

To my wife, Lisa, my gift from God and
co-adventurer on this journey called ministry.

And to my children, Emma, Addison, and Owen,
who inspire me to live like a kid every day and
to never lose sight of what matters most.

TEAM UP!

Foreword

I'm old enough to have seen an incredible maturing in youth ministry. I became a Christian and started in youth work during the "Jesus Movement"—a movement that changed the way churches did outreach and missions as well as youth and children's ministry. Today youth and children's ministry is a staple of every healthy, growing church. But long before even I was around, the pioneers of youth work led the way in warning the church to reach out to kids or risk losing them. Their message was prophetic.

When I came onto the youth ministry scene, books about youth ministry were just beginning to have a more practical focus. Many of us were still making things up as we went, but we were beginning to write down for others what we were doing. Some of the best youth ministry leadership was coming from outside the church through parachurch organizations, but people were rapidly taking that leadership into the church. Today, however, the youth and children's movement gets its leadership from within churches all over the world. And some of the strongest leadership voices are coming from outside the United States.

Now we're witnessing a brand-new movement of God called family ministry. Over a decade ago voices in leadership started talking about the need to partner with parents in youth and children's ministry. We knew the need was important, but very few had any idea how to do it. And the first books written on the subject were weak on offering practical advice, focusing more on declaring the need—just as the pioneers of youth work did in the early days of youth ministry.

Team Up! is a much-needed book written by someone who works in the church to make family ministry a reality every day. I remember well the first time I met my friend Phil Bell. What a voice! Even though he now lives in the United States, Phil has an incredible British accent. His voice is kind, positive, authentic, and caring, just as this book is. It's a practical book where you can find help on each page for implementing an effective family ministry in your church. Its message comes from the voice of a leader. And those who read it will find it to be incredibly helpful.

At HomeWord we have two sayings that get me going each day: "One of the major purposes of the church is to mentor parents; the parents mentor their children while partnering with the church, and the legacy of faith continues from generation to generation," and "When you reach the family, you reach the world." The family ministry movement is growing and changing even faster than youth and children's ministry did in its early days, with some family ministry conferences having larger attendance than conferences for youth and children's ministry. I'm thrilled for the new voices of leadership—such as Phil's—that are speaking into this ministry movement today.

Jim Burns, Ph.D.
President, HomeWord
Dana Point, California

Introduction

AN
UNPLANNED
JOURNEY

I have a confession. When I entered full-time ministry, I never really considered partnering with parents to be high on my priority list. I was committed to ministering to kids. Someone else could take care of the parents, right? On top of that, it wasn't long before I'd witnessed and experienced the pain of dealing with overly protective or critical parents in my ministry. From the parent who thought I only worked on Sundays to the parent who expected me to be on par with Jesus, it was easy to adopt a defensive approach to the parents I interacted with.

With those things in mind, I never saw the importance of expending energy to incorporate parents into my thinking and decisions. Typically, the average week of creating environments for kids and students provided me with enough to do. I didn't have time to add in communicating with and resourcing parents as well. I was barely treading water from week to week as it was. And what's more, why would I want to open myself up to parents, knowing that I might be criticized at some point?

Fifteen years ago I was forced to discover some solid answers to these kinds of questions. What I discovered wasn't what I was expecting, but I'm forever thankful for where those answers have taken me.

I know that partnering with parents can seem daunting and over-whelming, but I promise you that it's one of the greatest ways to reach and equip the next generation. In fact, let me be so bold as to say it this way: If you're not prepared to partner with parents, it's very likely your success in ministry will always be limited. So come on a journey with me and see why partnering with parents will increase your effectiveness in reaching and equipping the next generation for Christ. You won't regret it.

Where I've Been

I'm not from around these parts. I grew up in the bustling suburbs of London, England. In August 2000, I moved to Ann Arbor, Michigan. A few months prior, I'd been living and working in London as an insurance consultant while volunteering as a youth leader in my local church.

I had grown up outside the church. But thanks to my friend Andy Unwin, I was invited to an incredible youth group that forever changed my life. By the age of 18 I had accepted Christ at a youth workers' convention and was excited about pouring into the lives of young people. Looking back now, I realize that not only was God calling me to a new life in him, he was calling me into full-time ministry. It took another seven years to respond to that calling. But along the way I took some small steps as a volunteer, investing in kids just as some incredible adults had done for me in the years before. Over time I couldn't escape what God was calling me to, but I didn't quite know where to start. I didn't know, that is, until I spoke to Byron Porisch.

Byron was a 30-year veteran youth pastor who'd just been called to a large church to rebuild a struggling youth ministry that was once thriving. When I asked him for advice on where to start in pursuing God's call on my life, he gave me some incredible counsel and wisdom. Then he asked me a question that would change my life drastically: "What if you moved to the States and worked with me? I can show you how it's done, and maybe we can help you with your tuition?"

That was in May 2000. When I asked Byron for his advice, I never would have dreamed that I'd be changing careers and countries within a few short months. I arrived on a plane from England as a fresh-faced, 20-something Englishman with a plan to intern with Byron for four years

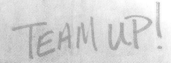

while studying youth ministry at a local Christian university. (Who in his right mind would agree to intern for four years? A fresh-faced Englishman, I guess.) At the time the university didn't offer a youth ministry degree, but rather a family life education degree. It was the closest thing to what I hoped to study, but I didn't really know what the degree program was all about. I was a little deflated that I couldn't study youth ministry, but I determined that my best education would come from being in the trenches of youth ministry with Byron anyway. In hindsight I'm thankful for this "plan B degree" that forever changed my thinking on how best to reach and equip the next generation for Christ. It's also what brought me into contact with "Prof" Ben.

I met Ben Freudenburg in the second year of my internship and studies. He arrived on campus straight out the trenches of family ministry and had written a book called *The Family-Friendly Church.* At the time, his book was already a few years old, but very few churches were even thinking about how to implement the kinds of things written on its pages. However, he'd been living and breathing family ministry for many years. He had a clear philosophy and was practical in his application.

Professor Ben is a pioneer in the family ministry movement. Much of his work has shaped the landscape of how churches can effectively reach the whole family. He was one of the first people to ask questions and provide answers about how church workers could continue their investment in kids while also employing a family-friendly strategy that empowered and equipped parents to be the primary influencers in their child's faith journey. Every class with Ben forced me to constantly evaluate how I was engaging parents in my ministry and how I could best equip them to continue the faith conversations and invest in their kids at home. How every calendar item, event, and program needed to consider parents first rather than as an afterthought. Ben's vision was to see parents as our primary ministry, and everything else would flow from there.

By the end of my four years with Byron and Ben, I had learned a great deal. Perhaps the greatest thing I learned was that the church is called to partner with parents to reach and equip the next generation. I had concluded that much of my ministry would only be putting out fires if I didn't invest in parents just as much as I invested in the kids I saw each week. And I was absolutely convinced that the days of running a "silo" ministry—seeing my ministry as the predominant way to effectively reach children and students and disregarding the role of parents or the importance of other ministries within the local church—could not continue. I could no longer send parents the unspoken message of "Drop your kids off and leave it to us." Though many parents saw it as my job to raise their kids in the faith, I came to see that it was my role to engage those parents and give them a new vision, strategy, and the practical steps to take.

Where We're Going

As a leader, your effectiveness in reaching and equipping the next generation for Christ will be greatest when you partner with parents and see them as co-laborers for the kingdom. It doesn't mean changing how you do your ministry entirely, but it will mean weaving some principles for partnering with parents into your existing day-to-day ministry. And that's actually great news for me and you. So many books give us ways to do ministry that are specific to a particular context and require us to clone our ministries after them. My hope is that after reading this book you can keep your ministry identity intact while more effectively partnering with parents and reaching the next generation for Christ.

It's also my hope that your church's governing body and the other leaders in your church will read this book. Not only will it help them see the need to give greater focus to partnering with parents, but it will also help them find strategic and practical ideas to implement this philosophy and strategy into the life of the whole church. As a children's or youth ministry worker, take the time to grab a coffee with the influencers and decision-makers in your church and talk with them about the thoughts in this book. It just might be a game changer for them, too.

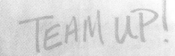

Author's Note

A couple of things to keep in mind as you read:

First, at the time I wrote this book I was the family ministries pastor at a church in Michigan. Between that time and the release of the book, I moved with my family to North Carolina to take on the same role at a different church. Any mentions in the book of my present ministry setting are in reference to the church in Michigan.

Second, I occasionally make mention of people in my past and present ministries who illustrate the principles or ideas in this book. In some cases you will see an asterisk following their names, indicating that those names have been changed to protect the privacy of those individuals.

Chapter 1

THE **NEED** FOR **PARTNERING**

Hint: It's not about your ministry.

I grew up in England. As a kid I was always enthralled by the sport of rowing. Every year around Easter, I would sit in front of the TV and watch the Oxford and Cambridge Boat Race. These incredible teams would work together to be the first along approximately four miles of the River Thames in West London. The event is a huge deal on the British sporting calendar and is often watched by over 200,000 spectators along the riverfront. Most years this race is hotly contested and usually provides a tantalizing finish in the last mile, with the honors switching between Oxford and Cambridge from year to year.

There are usually three components that make for a winning rowing team. First, the team needs great strength and endurance to last throughout the entire race. Second, it's the rowers' efficiency in moving the oars in the water that helps the boat glide seamlessly through the water. Third— and perhaps most important—is the synchronization of the team. It has to work together in perfect unison so that each oar hits the water at the same time and in the same way.

So what does that have to do with reaching and equipping the next generation for Christ?

Many churches today are out of sync when it comes to the way we approach children's and student ministries. While some of the oars may be working to propel the team forward, others are going into the water at odd angles or not at all as they try to deal with the most pressing concerns of the moment. Churches recruit and resource staff and volunteers based on those most pressing needs and not based on winning the race. As a result, these ministries are falling behind.

For the most part, churches tailor their services and programs based on the felt needs of the people coming in their doors. Whatever is the latest and biggest problem will get the most attention and investment. As a result, we tend to give most of our time, energy, and resources to issues that kids are struggling with in the moment rather than helping them to prevent those issues from coming up in the first place. Don't get me wrong—investing in children's and youth ministry programs to meet the real and pressing needs of modern-day families is important. And it's something the church has done extremely well. But there needs to be something more.

Helping Parents Win the Race

Let's be honest. Parenting in our world today is a scary prospect and isn't for cowards. Headlines are continually dominated by suicides, bullying, addictions, and the advancement of an overly sexualized culture. In recent years we've also seen greater pressure for parents to succeed financially as the world has walked precariously through recession. The demands on the modern family have left many parents with limited time and resources to raise their kids, and they're looking to the church to help them.

Many parents are living in constant survival mode. Some are facing the realities of adolescence. They're watching their kids struggle through a multitude of potentially life-altering issues and feel completely inept at dealing with a fast-moving youth culture. Parents are watching the race get away from them, and they're not sure how to catch up, much less get out ahead.

As I sat in a local coffeehouse writing this chapter, I saw a friend who is the senior pastor of a nearby church. I asked him how his church was doing, and his response confirmed my premise: "What draws people to

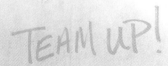

most churches is crisis and kids. You've either got to meet a need that someone is facing or give people a place that'll be good for their kids." While we both agreed that there are many additional reasons why families might choose a good church, ultimately their choice will be swayed by whether their felt needs are being met and if there's a quality children's and youth ministry. Parents will tolerate a mediocre church service if they feel their kids are having an incredible experience in the children's or youth ministry. In response, churches have improved their youth and children's ministry programs to attract parents who are desperate for help.

In a parenting seminar offered by HomeWord called *Generation 2 Generation*, Dr. Jim Burns points to the foundations of youth ministry in the local church today. Many churches adopted an approach that was developed out the success of Young Life and Youth for Christ in the 1970s. Churches saw the great success of these parachurch organizations and their ability to attract greater numbers. Now for nearly half a century, we've seen a greater level of investment in youth and children's ministry as churches have recruited qualified ministry workers, purchased the latest curriculums, and created exciting ministry environments for kids.

In my experience the church that provides a great children's and youth ministry will attract and keep the greater number of families. As I've talked with parents over the years, it's been interesting to hear why they've chosen a particular church. Many have been honest enough to say that their choice was not for themselves, but to get their kids engaged in a children's or youth ministry that would help their kids connect to other Christian kids and grow in Christ. At a previous church one mom told me, "The worship service here is not what we enjoy, but we love the youth ministry here and we want to see our kids get plugged in. If they love it here, we'll get past our own preferences."

Keeping a Straight Line

As you read this you might wondering, "Is he going to to drop the hammer on children's and youth ministry? Is he about to say that meeting a family's needs is a problem? Is he against churches creating engaging environments where their kids can learn and grow in Christ in a way that's developmentally appropriate?" Certainly not!

I, too, want my kids to be part of vibrant children's and youth ministries. I want them to drag me to church and talk my ear off on the way home about how God has captured their hearts because of what they heard and experienced at church. I want to hear them tell me how they served and how their lives were changed because of it. I want them to experience what I experienced all those years ago growing up in England, where my heart was opened to the gospel because of an incredible youth ministry. I want them to have other adults invest in their lives the way John Powell, Patrick Horgan, Roger Gammon, Kate Dean, and Tim Lee invested in my life and helped me find Christ in the midst of a messy adolescence.

I believe in children's and youth ministries to the core of who I am. But that's only one side of the boat. And when you only use the oars on one side, you just go in circles. You have to work the oars on both sides of the boat to make any progress.

There will always be a need for the church to provide outstanding ministry environments for children and youth. But there's also a need to partner with parents at the same time. In the past few decades there's been an imbalance in how much time we've spent responding to the immediate needs of kids compared with the time we've spent investing in and preparing parents as the primary influencers in their child's faith journey. If you don't agree, just look at the job postings for children's and youth ministry positions. Most likely you'll find little to no emphasis on partnering with parents. And when it is mentioned, it'll probably be a vague reference at best.

I was recently struck by this imbalance at a national conference that has a "family ministry" emphasis. Despite its vision to partner with parents, I seldom heard about it from the main stage or in the breakout sessions. Rather, they defaulted back to talking about the nuts and bolts of what we as children's and youth workers do with our kids and students. And while what we do is extremely important, if that's all we focus on, there's a gigantic piece missing that has astronomical and eternal implications.

Partnering with parents needs to be woven into the very fabric of what we're doing in our children's and youth ministries. The most successful churches will balance it with providing kids a great, Jesus-centered experience. When that happens, they become part of a team that successfully moves things forward.

Heading for the Right Finish

So we don't miss the most important point of all, let's be clear that partnering with parents and providing effective ministries to children and youth is not just about helping our kids get through the challenges they'll face in childhood and adolescence. Our ultimate goal needs to always be reaching and equipping them with the gospel of Jesus Christ. It's that foundation of faith that will best enable them to navigate through the inevitable challenges of life.

Rick Lawrence makes a similar point in his book *Jesus-Centered Youth Ministry*:

> "Up until now most of us have been like overworked pruners in a fast-growing orchard. We scurry around trying to cut off the bad fruit we see around us…The truth is, as kids come to know Jesus more deeply and begin to abide in him more deeply and begin to abide in him as the 'root' of their life, their fruit will change. They will be transformed 'by the renewing of [their] mind' (Romans 12:2). We won't have to run around cutting off rotten fruit!"

I wholeheartedly agree. And I'd like to weave in an additional thought: Helping kids and students know Jesus more deeply happens best when parents are empowered to be the primary ones equipping their kids for their faith journeys. It's not that you and I stop sharing the gospel with kids or providing excellent environments for them. It's that we need to intentionally focus on setting parents up to become the spiritual heroes in their kids' lives. Equipping parents to raise their kids with a Jesus-centered foundation will result in their kids being better equipped to face the challenges of today and tomorrow.

Getting All the Oars In

One of the most common objections I hear from other children's and youth pastors often goes something like this: "I know I need to partner with parents, but what if they don't want to partner with me?" It's a fair question. Many parents are disengaged, having a "drop off" mentality where they see us as the experts who'll save their kids. But in some cases, they're simply too busy keeping up with life. Partnering with you and me is often just one more thing to add to their already hectic schedules. What's more, many of the families we serve are already consumed with helping their kids deal with some kind of pressing issue. In those cases we need to see parents not as disengaged so much as being engaged somewhere else, and it's our role to help them bring an urgency and attention to engaging with their children's faith journey.

It's our job to sound the alarm—to alert parents to the difficulties their kids may face now and in the future. Doing so is a key to grabbing their attention. The more parents can understand about what's ahead, the greater the likelihood they'll make a priority of investing in their child's spiritual journey now. But our role is not simply to scare the life out of parents by exposing them to the potential struggles their kids will face now and in the future. Rather, it's to educate them regarding those issues. Doing so is often the catalyst for parents making changes in the way they raise their kids in the faith.

For any good communicator, it's crucial to get the audience's attention at the beginning of a message by stirring up a sense of need. It's no different when you're dealing with parents. Some of us are grabbing the attention of children and students on a weekly basis, but we don't realize the need to grab the attention of parents by sounding the alarm on the issues their kids are facing. Once we have their attention, it's more likely they'll take time to listen to someone like you or me who can partner with them and equip them to equip their children with the life-changing gospel.

In his book *Soul Searching: The Religious and Spiritual Lives of American Teenagers*, Dr. Christian Smith provides extensive research surrounding the spiritual habits and influences in the lives of teenagers. What he's found is that while culture often downplays the influence of parents in the lives of their children, parents actually have the greatest influence—and therefore the greatest ability—to shape the spiritual lives of their children. Parents are with their kids substantially more than you and I and therefore have a greater overall potential to influence their children's faith journey. It's the way God designed it to be. If we're lucky we might get a couple of hours a week with the average child or student who attends our church. Between mealtimes, car journeys, vacations, school events, and hang-out times, imagine how many more hours the average parent has

compared to that. Imagine how many more teachable moments that provides parents compared with what you and I have. Think of what would happen if we were to support parents by equipping and empowering them to make greater use of those times to instill faith into their kids' lives. You and I have limited potential when we focus only on what happens at church. However, there is massive potential when we emphasize what happens at home as well.

Moving Ahead One Stroke at a Time

"But how can I give parents practical help?" If you haven't asked that question yet, I'm sure you will soon. In my early days of ministry, I knew I was meant to partner with parents, but with the exception of a few authors and organizations, there were very few resources to help. There are still only a few resources that provide practical how to's for reaching, equipping, and partnering with parents. Many of those that do exist are program specific and leave me feeling as if I have to change my ministry and become a clone of some megachurch in a totally different context. I often walk away from those kinds of resources feeling like they've provided very little in the way of rubber-meets-the-road ideas, strategies, or steps.

This is a practical how-to book that's not program specific. Whether you're in ministry full- or part-time or you're a volunteer, these ideas can be woven into your ministry at your own pace. I know I get frustrated when I read books or go to a conference that requires me to overhaul my whole ministry to make a new strategy work. The good news is that this book won't require you to do that. It might require you to add some components or reassign some resources, but you won't have to change everything you do. And here's the best news: You won't have to spend thousands of dollars on an expensive new curriculum either.

The ideas contained here can be implemented as you read and as you lead in your context. The first part of the book is focused on understanding what's gone before us so we can look ahead to the future. So much of what we do in the local church had a starting place, yet many of us have come through the church and never sought to understand where we've come from or why we do what we do. The rest of the book gives insights and practical steps that can be implemented immediately in most contexts. As you read, take time to pause and consider how you can weave those things into your ministry. At the end of every chapter are questions to answer and action steps to take that will help you do just that.

That being said, a word of warning is also due: Don't try to change the world overnight. Begin with some easy wins and go from there. Changing the culture of a church and the mindsets of parents can and will take time. It's important that you take small steps as you solidify your thoughts on partnering with parents, and then implement changes out of your convictions. Since there's still a potential for big changes in your ministry, it's helpful for everyone around you to experience one step at a time. That'll make a huge difference in the long term. In my experience, change comes best by employing a strategy of small steps that make a marked difference over time. Not only are small steps easier to manage on your part, but they'll always be easier for people around you to stomach.

A while ago I sat down with a group of youth workers in a local restaurant as part of a networking meeting. As we enjoyed lunch together, we began to discuss ideas and resources with one another. I always love hearing what other churches are doing and seeing what ideas I could use in my context. As we shared ideas, the topic of partnering with parents came up and we began to discuss ways in which to engage parents in our respective ministries. But as we navigated the conversation, it was clear to me that there was a disparity in what we saw as partnering with parents. One youth worker clearly indicated that, for him, partnering with parents was focused on recruiting parents to help him with his ministry and involving them in his organization. While this is indeed a step to partnering with parents, it was obviously what his emphasis was all about.

Let me be clear. This book is not about providing you with ways to get parents to do stuff for you in your ministry or support your vision. Rather, this book is about helping you partner with parents so that you can support them in pursuing a biblical vision to reach and equip the next generation for Christ.

So are you ready? Grab a cup of tea (remember, I am English), and let's dive into this together.

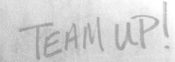

Chapter 2

IT **STARTS** WITH **YOU**

How your example can make or break your ability to partner with parents.

I t was a conversation that would forever change my marriage and my ministry. As I sat next to my wife, Lisa, tears trickled down our faces. The once-new couch we'd bought when we got married was no longer comfortable and was falling apart. In the past year our torn and tattered couch had become a reflection of our lives in ministry. On this particular day, the pain of loss only amplified the messiness of marriage and ministry.

Like many couples, we were navigating the immense pain of miscarriage. As tears flowed I was struck by just how quickly my soft-spoken wife was able to articulate her feelings and emotions. In the past I'd learned to wait for her to talk, and sometimes it could mean waiting a few days before I really heard and understood her heart. But this day was different from others as she talked openly about our grief and the pain of our loss. As we talked together, it was as if the loss of our baby had allowed us to capture what was most important in our lives. In his book *The Problem of Pain,* C.S Lewis said, "God whispers to us in our pleasures, speaks in our conscience, but shouts in our pains: it is His megaphone to rouse a deaf world." That was true for us on this day. We experienced God's comfort. But we also experienced incredible clarity.

"If you never did ministry again, I don't think I would care." As the words came out of Lisa's mouth, I didn't feel the need to push back or clarify what she meant. I wasn't devastated by her words. I didn't need to look her in the eyes and wonder where such a thought came from. I didn't fall off the couch in surprise. I knew exactly what she was thinking and feeling. I instantly knew why she needed to speak in such a direct way.

The Problem

I had a dream job in ministry: build a youth ministry from the ground up, design it how I wanted, and share in the fruit of a fast-growing church plant. If you've ever been involved in a church plant, you know that it's easy to wear many hats; and if you're not careful, it's easy to sacrifice yourself and your family without realizing it. That was the case for Lisa and me. And as a result, the dream quickly became a nightmare. What was once a blessing now felt more like a curse.

The hard but honest words my Lisa spoke hit home as she shared her frustrations of being married to an overscheduled, unhealthy youth pastor. It wasn't like I didn't see it coming. Over many months I had blurred the lines of ministry and family. I'd created an unhealthy ministry schedule in a church that was exploding with growth. My overscheduled ministry had become the enemy of my faith walk, my family, my health, and my relationships. We looked around and realized we had little time for friends. We were isolated and alone. In the midst of a miscarriage, we were broken, discouraged, and our dream had been lost. We had crashed, and we were hurting.

The Need

No one ever thinks it'll happen to them. No one sets off in ministry planning to burn out. In the midst of it all, part of me was in denial. But another part of me knew there were things I needed to change. I'd been to conferences that told me to set boundaries and create balance. I knew some simple changes would make all the difference, but I was allowing the complexity of ministry to lead the way.

I couldn't blame the church. And even though I often blamed the people who were leading me, it was ultimately my fault for not defining

 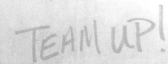

the boundaries for my life and ministry more clearly. Every time I said yes to being at church was time missed with my family. It took the hard but necessary words of my wife and the pain of a miscarriage to shake me back to reality. It was time to dream again. Time to create a vision for our family and ministry.

In the next year I embarked on a journey of change that would result in a change of priorities and a change of churches. It was extremely painful to leave a church and group of people I loved. But I've never regretted taking the opportunity to rediscover what it means to make my family my first and primary ministry. I wish I could tell you that I've gotten it all figured out since then, but there are still times I realize that I've said yes to too many things. Fortunately, Lisa and I have learned to communicate better and have established a healthier balance between family and ministry. And ultimately we've seen God bless both our family and ministry as we've sought his best for both.

The Answer

The way you invest in your own family will significantly affect the fruit of your ministry. To be more specific, you can't expect to see fruit in your ministry if there's no fruit at home. Let that reality sink in for a moment. It's easy to agree with it on the surface. But consider the ripple effect it can have in our lives and ministries.

Whether you're single or married, young or old; whether you're a rookie or have years of experience, your example will always speak louder than your words. If you truly want to attract and influence other families, the vision, priorities, and foundations you live out in your family must be distinctly different from the harassed and stressed world that you live in. I'm not saying you have to be perfect at it. But we live in a world in which talk is cheap. Over time our ability to influence others is diminished when they see that our lives are in conflict with the message that we preach.

The Challenge

"Keep putting into practice all you learned and received from me—everything you heard from me and saw me doing. Then the God of peace will be with you" (Philippians 4:9).

Imagine being one of the Christians in Philippi reading Paul's letter and remembering all that he taught you. And as if his teaching wasn't enough, you remember his example, too. It was his teaching and example together that let him say, "Whatever you heard from me is only part of the picture. Look at how I lived the truth, too. Then go and live it out yourself. You know it's the real deal."

Despite a little embellishment on my part, I think you get the idea. And here's what's imperative to understand as it relates to partnering with parents: Partnering begins with how you invest in your own family first. Your teaching and instruction must be seen in how you personally live out your faith in your family. It needs to be an overflow of who you are. That's what'll make you a lighthouse for the watching world.

The way we invest in our own families is the most attractive reason for parents to follow our leadership. As parents engage in defensive battles related to their kids, they're looking for hope and direction from people who are successfully defending their own families. It stands to reason that you wouldn't make a financial investment with someone who has a track record of wasting his or her own money. In the same way, parents won't listen to you and me if we're not passionately pursuing a healthy family life ourselves. That's true for us if we're single or married and whether we have kids or not. Our example is the greatest tool we have to influence the people who are looking to follow our lead. Your investment in your family will have a greater long-term effect than some of the most innovative programs and ministries you can create. And if you fail to invest in your own family first, there's far more at stake than just your ministry.

The Goal

If you talk to my wife, Lisa, she'll affirm that I'm not Jesus. The good news is, that's not the goal. It's not about being perfect (or appearing to

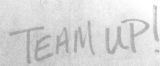

be perfect). It's about authentically pursuing God's best for your family. In fact, I would go so far as to say that the rough edges of your family will put others at ease when they realize you're just like them. Who wants to follow a perfect family anyway? I sure can't measure up to that standard.

A few years ago I wrote a blog post about the importance of balancing family and ministry *(philbell.me/2009/07/13/balancing-family-ministry)*. I made the case that investing in our families has to happen before we can leave a lasting impact on our ministries. At the time I thought this was a clear-cut argument that everyone would be quick to agree with. After receiving a few emails and a couple of comments, I came to realize how naïve it was to assume that this was a given for the readers of my blog. Since then I've come to see a dichotomy between those who balance family and ministry and those who don't. I've observed those who have ensured the health of their families came first—and as a result their ministries were healthy, too. On the other hand, I've watched some people sacrifice their families for ministry at a huge cost, not only to their families, but to their present ministries and their long-term effectiveness as well. My hope for you is that this chapter will prompt you to consider the health of your family (or future family) and evaluate the example you're setting for those you lead.

The Bible

Ministry is a calling and requires us to make sacrifices at times. However, a quick look at Scripture will help us balance that out. In 1 Timothy 3:1-3, Paul instructs Timothy regarding the requirements for church leaders:

> "This is a trustworthy saying: 'If someone aspires to be an elder, he desires an honorable position.' So an elder must be a man whose life is above reproach. He must be faithful to his wife. He must exercise self-control, live wisely, and have a good reputation. He must enjoy having guests in his home, and he must be able to teach. He must not be a heavy drinker or be violent. He must be gentle, not quarrelsome, and not love money."

For a young leader like Timothy, it was crucial to hear Paul explain what to look for in leaders who would leave a lasting legacy and have an effective ministry in the church. Timothy was in Ephesus. And in the Ephesian church at that time, many of the current and potential leaders were being sucked into unhealthy habits by the Greco-Roman influences of the day. The culture was extremely narcissistic. Status and power were sought at any cost. Many church leaders were falling into sin and accepting false teaching. There was plenty of opportunity for the leaders of that day to get swept away by a sea of self-focus and allow the waves of unhealthy habits to swallow them up, even where their families were concerned. Consequently, Paul knew that leaders would need to be solid in their faith and conduct, including in the ways they managed their families.

Take a moment to consider the world you and I live in now. It's not all that different in terms of the priorities and values Timothy had to deal with in the church at Ephesus. We still see leaders fall into the traps of status, power, and striving for significance. Consider some of the other traps you and I fall into as we try to minister to those around us:

- **We focus on pleasing people.** We live to make others happy instead of pleasing God first. We say yes to everyone and everything and feel ashamed at the thought of saying no. In the meantime we become worn out, and ministry loses its joy and excitement. We run on empty and give our families our leftovers—if there's anything left to give.

- **We build platforms.** We attempt to build a platform of influence for ourselves and leave little to no room on the platform for Christ. We're constantly fueled by the accolades of success and trying to make a name for ourselves.

- **We mistake our identities.** We base our identities on what we do rather than who we are in Christ. Rather than being confident in the person God has made us to be, we're caught up in the position we hold.

- **We break boundaries.** We don't say no to ministry needs, yet we constantly say no to time with and focus on our families. We see it as the easier route, expecting our families to be more understanding than our senior pastors or congregations.

- **We lose our devotional lives.** We let our study time for ministry become a substitute for our personal devotional time. We let reading God's

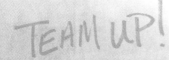

Word and applying it personally and practically get replaced by lesson preparation for the benefit of others.

- **We ignore worship.** We let the corporate worship experience become a distant memory as we look to serve others and ensure that everything depends on us. We encourage families to sit together in church, but our own families haven't had that experience for a long time.

- **We aren't fully present.** Rather than shutting off our technological gadgets at strategic times, we convince ourselves that every phone call, text message, email, and social media request has to be answered right away. We send our kids and spouses the message that the outside world is more important than they are.

- **We ignore our physical health.** We don't take time to exercise, and we let food become a source of comfort, which leads to health complications over time. We lack energy and always feel like we need more sleep (which is very possible). We're told that the body is the temple of the Holy Spirit, yet for some of us it feels like the temple is crumbling.

After giving Timothy the list of prerequisites for church leaders, Paul builds the bridge between who a person is at home and who he or she is as a church leader:

> "He must manage his own family well, having children who respect and obey him. For if a man cannot manage his own household, how can he take care of God's church?" (1 Timothy 3:4-5)

And there it is—the crucial connection between how we minister to our own families at home and our ministry to the church. It's also the foundation for how we partner with parents. If you and I don't know how to invest in our own families first, we can't begin to understand how to invest in others' families.

GAME PLAN SUMMARY

The way you invest in your own family will significantly affect the influence you have with parents.

TEAM UP!

PRACTICE DRILLS

*Use the following action steps to help you apply
what you've learned to your life and ministry.*

1. In the next 24 hours, take time to journal about your faith, your family, and your ministry. How do you think others view your family? Is your family life and your personal walk with God a light in the darkness for others to follow? How do you match up to the kind of leader Paul told Timothy to look for in 1 Timothy 3? What has God been bringing to your attention as you've read this chapter?

2. Identify one or two areas of your faith or family life that need attention. Create one attainable goal for each of those areas that'll help you bring them to the forefront of your ministry.

3. Contact two or three key people who'll give you an honest assessment of how well you're prioritizing your family and your walk with God. Set up a time to talk about what they see, and ask them to hold you accountable for making positive changes in any areas of potential growth they see.

4. Ask a close friend, mentor, or accountability partner to discuss any unhealthy motives or habits you can relate to. Ask that person to walk alongside you as you work to eradicate those things from your life and ministry.

5. Create a vision statement for your family. If you're married, be sure to include your spouse in the process. A good vision statement paints a picture of a hoped-for future. Take time to pray and dream about it, and make sure your statement reflects a healthy balance between God, family, and ministry.

TEAM UP!

Chapter 3

BUILD A UNIFIED TEAM

Work past your own hesitations and understand the parents you're partnering with.

W e're called to be on the same team as we reach the next generation for Christ. But let's face it—parents can sometimes be scary figures to deal with. Partnering with parents can be painful and can leave the strongest of leaders with scars and insecurities. Is it any wonder why so many youth and children's workers avoid certain parents or avoid parents entirely?

If you've been in ministry for a while, you probably have some stories and possibly some scars that have been caused by a parent lashing out. In my early days of ministry it was relatively easy to avoid dealing with parents, as I was an intern who lived under the protection of the full-time paid guy. If I ran good programs and communicated well, parents would be happy with me—for the most part. But it wasn't long before I was under the microscope and under the scrutiny of a few parents who didn't like a decision I'd made. I eventually discovered the pain of being told, "Parents are talking, and they don't like what you're doing with their kids." Then I'd have to sit across the table from a parent who was questioning why I wasn't doing more for the ministry and their child in particular. I soon began to see parents as the enemy, with my default being to be on the defensive. And if the best defense is offense, it didn't take long until I went on the attack.

In the midst of criticism or failure, I could easily point out the flaws in particular parents and blame them for the damage I had to "clean up" in their kids' lives. Every time I went to a conference I would hear (and share) stories of problem parents and hurt feelings. At times my encounters with parents caused me to wonder if ministry was even worth the effort. Sadly, my wife, Lisa, would hear some of the rants that came out of my mouth in those moments of hurt and frustration:

> "These people care about sports more than they care about Jesus. Why don't they make their kids' faith journey a priority? They want me to lead their kids to Christ, yet they don't seem to be doing anything at home."

I could go on and on, but you get the point. I'm not trying to get you all riled up. Rather, I'm just trying to help you know you're not alone. Many of us have stories of conflicts we've had with parents in our ministries. If you don't have stories already, you probably will at some point. You and I are broken people with insecurities, as are parents—who are on the same team as we are. As a team we're called to reach and equip the next generation for Christ. The devil would love to create team disunity since he knows it's effective in stifling the vision that we as a team need desperately to hold on to.

Understanding the Players

David* had only been in ministry for a short time and was nearly ready to throw in the towel when I spoke to him a few years ago. As a young married guy in a new church, he'd arrived with a great deal of zeal and purpose. Within a year he was tired and depleted by a small group of critical parents. As a new leader, he admitted he made too many changes at once, but he also acknowledged that his communication skills were not the best. Before he knew it, parents were talking to his pastor and he was beginning to hear about their frustrations second hand. The pressure was mounting, and it seemed an insurmountable task to win back the favor of the parents.

34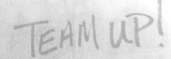

If you're like David or me, there are days you just want to disengage from the pain of partnering with parents. But in those moments it's essential that you and I face a reality: Our effectiveness in reaching and equipping the next generation is limited only if we fail to understand parents and involve them in our thinking, planning, and implementation. By shifting our focus from seeing parents as opponents to be beaten to seeing them as teammates to win alongside of, we increase our effectiveness in ministry.

While I can't control how parents act or react toward me as a leader, I've discovered that listening to them and finding understanding is the best start I can make. However, while we might be good at understanding children and students, many of us aren't very good at understanding parents. Part of the reason for this is we don't take time to truly listen to parents.

Before I had kids of my own, I often found it challenging to understand where parents were coming from. I didn't take time to listen. And honestly, I didn't see the importance. It wasn't hard for me to relate to David, since I used to be just like him.

During those years before Lisa and I started a family, I asked some supportive parents to become my eyes and ears and a sounding board for what I was thinking and planning. More than anything I wanted to cut down on the potential for criticism by running ideas past parents first, but I also discovered some key insights from some honest and vulnerable parents. Many of these discussions gave me an inside track to the life of parents who came through our church doors every weekend. Then when I eventually had my own kids, it gave me even greater insight to the joys and struggles experienced by parents. As I began to see parents differently, I began to minister to them differently. And the way I view parents today has greatly influenced my efforts and increased my effectiveness, too.

Reading the Roster

For the remainder of this chapter, it's my goal to give you a snapshot of some of the parents in your ministry. While we can't talk about every kind of parent in your ministry, it's my hope that God will give you some greater perspective into their lives and the worlds in which they live. My hope is that if you see them as an opponent today, you'll see them as being on the same team tomorrow.

Distracted Parents First of all, it's imperative that we realize our perception of parents isn't always accurate. We see this best when we consider what it's like to walk a mile in their shoes. As I've leaned in and listened to the heart of parents, I've often found them to be more distracted than they are disengaged. They're either distracted by living in survival mode, or they're consumed with well-intentioned pursuits that they hope will bring success for their kids. And where disengaged parents are often hard to reach, distracted parents can be won over. Begin by seeing parents as distracted rather than being disengaged, and from there take the time to truly understand the distractions and challenges they're facing.

Overwhelmed Parents Many parents are living in survival mode. In recent years parents have been forced to make decisions that take time away from the family in order to pay the bills. A Pew Research Center study shows that over half the parents with children under the age of 18 find it a challenge to balance family and work. The same study confirmed that between 34 and 40 percent of parents feel constantly rushed. In their harried situations, they don't know where to begin when it comes to investing in their kids spiritually. But most parents would never want to admit that to you and me. After all, people in the church are supposed to have it all together, aren't we? Even if someone had a good role model growing up, there are many times questions about whether he or she is making a difference creep in. (I know this to be true for Lisa and me. There are times I've had to hold on to the words of my mentor Ron, who told me to "stay the course and be consistent even when you feel like it's not working.")

Helicopter Parents Helicopter parents hover over their kids' lives every moment of every day in an attempt to see them be successful and protect them from any kind of harm. They want to be there to support their kids and ensure their kids are well-rounded and set up for success.

On the good side, helicopter parents want to be involved with and actively participate in their children's lives. I've seen this to be true in the last decade, as much larger numbers of parents want to volunteer in the ministries their kids attend. They're also open and receptive to helping their kids grow in the faith. However, it's also possible for helicopter parents to be overly involved and stifling to their kids. In their attempt to give their kids the best opportunities for the future, they can also push their children to succeed and fill their schedules with all kinds of extracurricular activities

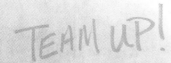

that'll one day look good on a college application. Often this kind of focus can lead to their kids not having ownership and a say in their future—or in their faith journey. Eventually when they leave the house for college or career, their kids can seem to wander in their faith and in their lives.

If there's a way these parents could be seen as disengaged, it's in the way they prioritize their children's faith. They're so busy making sure their children don't miss out on opportunities to advance socially, academically, or in any other way the parents see as important that their child's spiritual growth can fall to the wayside. So often it's not that they don't care, it's simply that they don't see the importance. They have great intentions but the wrong priorities.

When we see ourselves as being on the same team as helicopter parents, we can offer them support and help redirect their efforts. We can channel their motives into a greater focus on reaching and equipping their kids for the faith journey.

Single Parents According to the Kids Count Data Center, 35 percent of all children in the United States live in single-parent families. While that figure could vary depending on a variety of factors, the point is that many of the parents in your ministry could be single parents who are trying to manage a house, a job, and raising their kids to be happy and healthy. Given the load they carry on a daily basis, they already see you as a partner, but only in a partial sense. You're the one who gives their kids a place to go to and have fun while learning about God. You give them a break from their kids for an hour or two a week, allowing them to attend church or get their grocery shopping done while their kids are at youth group.

These are also the parents who may give you a hard time if you ever cancel youth group or take a break for a week or two. For them, it's a huge deal to find an alternative event to occupy their kids. Don't take it personally if they're abrupt with you at times. It's not that they mean to come across as self-focused or critical; they simply can't see beyond their harried life that's teetering on a tipping point. In my experience with single parents, there's often a story of regret concerning their kids that they carry around with them. The fact that they're at your church is huge, since being at church with people "who have it all together" is a painful reminder of their struggles. A few years ago, a woman I'll call Kerry shared with me how she always felt accepted and welcome at church, but personally she struggled with the stigma of being a single mom at church. Since then I've met many more single parents who have communicated the same struggles and insecurities.

Because single parents already see you as a partner in helping them with their kids, it's crucial that we help them see the greater scope of how we can be on their team. So often their schedule is the hardest part about being able to come alongside them, so it's crucial to overcommunicate the calendar and to ensure that we offer them support at times they're naturally and normally at church.

Special Needs Parents In my time in ministry, I've never seen so many children with special needs as I see at my present church. A few years ago we decided to put a stake in the ground and commit to reaching and equipping families who have children with special needs. There are times I've gotten teary-eyed watching our children with special needs as they engage their peers and adult buddies in our children's and student ministries. I'm also moved when I see their parents (some of whom are single parents) who are steadfastly committed to them in every way. I try to imagine what their day-to-day world is like, and I can barely fathom how they cope. "But by the grace of God and his enormous strength" is what one parent told me a while ago.

As I've talked with parents who have children with special needs, I've come to realize that not only is their world constantly demanding, but many of them have not always seen the church as a place of support and hope. This makes my heart heavy, and it should. Recently a mom who leads a group for parents of children with special needs shared these valuable but heart-rending insights with me:

> "We never have a minute to ourselves, and it's hard to invest in other key relationships when I have to be focused on caring for our child with special needs. We're always *that* parent with *that* kid. It's hard to come to church since many churches don't understand or know what to do for our kids and us. In 20 years this is the first church where I've experienced this kind of care and concern. I wish we could have found a place like this for my son when he was young."

 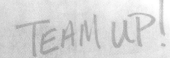

It's my hope that, as I have, you'll develop a heart for these families who traditionally haven't found a place to belong in most churches.

While I could go on with other categories of parents you and I see every week, for now I hope that what I have provided serves as a snapshot to get you thinking about parents and help you better understand their worlds. It's certainly easier to see ourselves as being on the same team with parents when we've taken time to understand more and assume less.

Unifying the Team

Being on the same team with parents isn't rocket science. There are some universal principles that go a long way to partnering with them and allowing them to see us as being on the same team. They begin with the simple actions of praying, listening, understanding, and involving.

Praying Prayer is such a simple thing to do, but I've found that the busyness of ministry means I often don't take time to pray for the ones I minister to—especially parents. While I might make time to pray for kids, it has taken work to get into the habit of regularly praying for parents. And as I've developed that habit, I've learned that I need to not only pray for parents as they raise their kids, I need to ask God to give me insight into parents' lives and wisdom to see how I can best support them. It seems simple, but it's incredibly powerful when you and I take time to seek God's wisdom.

Listening Listening is a doorway to trust and partnering with parents, but sadly it's often disregarded in the busyness of our ministry schedules. When we take time to listen, we communicate care and concern for the parents who are on our team. It doesn't have to be a major undertaking. It can happen in the lobby of your church or when parents pick up their children at the end of programmed ministry times. Asking parents about their week, how their kids are doing, and how you can pray for them is a great place to begin. If you're a leader of a ministry, it's essential that you have volunteers who enable you to be free to talk with parents as they drop off or pick up their kids. You can't be so busy doing things with kids that you have no time to engage with and listen to parents. If you're a volunteer and don't have any other adults to hand responsibilities off to, it'll mean consciously balancing your contact time with kids and parents. Don't try to get to every parent every week; begin by seeking out one good conversation a week with a parent. Even one conversation each week will help you build trust and better understand the hearts of the parents you minister to.

Understanding Not only will parents trust you when you listen, but you'll gain understanding that helps you see parents differently. In my early years of ministry, I spent too much time talking to parents, trying to show them what I knew. In more recent years, I've taken greater time to listen to and learn from parents, trying to get a better understanding of where they're at. Whether it's through a face-to-face conversation or through surveys, it's essential to understand parents' worlds and how you can support them as they reach and equip their children.

Involving Earlier I referred to recruiting some parents to be my eyes and ears in ministry. I wanted these parents to be sounding boards for my decisions, hoping they could help me avert poor decisions and improve what I was doing—which they did. They became the catalysts for some of my best ideas and helped me to avoid potential disasters in scheduling and programming. As with many of my plans, however, I discovered that God had a greater purpose in mind. As I got to know and love those parents, they also became my allies, my advocates, and they gave me a better perspective on the things we discussed.

Let's take a moment to consider those benefits to listening to, understanding, and involving parents.

We gain allies. When all is said and done, the most important aspect of being on the same team as parents is the result we all experience together. As we'll see in the chapter on vision, we're called to partner with parents to reach the next generation for Christ. When we work as a team toward this vision, we see greater things happen in the lives of children and students in our ministries. It means we have to swallow our pride at times, but some of the best solutions I've seen have come from the wisdom of parents who feel as if they're part of the team and who sense a real ownership of what we're trying to accomplish together.

We gain advocates. No matter what we do, there will always be criticism from parents. Don't forget, many of them are harried, overwhelmed, and insecure (just like you and me). When we receive criticism, it's essential that you and I have a team of parents we can listen to and talk

 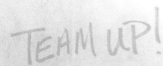

with about what we're planning and doing. The members of that team can become great advocates for us. As parents, they're well positioned to represent us to other parents who don't yet see the big picture or might have misunderstood our intentions.

A few years ago, a parent misunderstood some decisions I'd made in the student ministry. In between church services, I had one of those awkward conversations with a parent who was clearly incensed with my decisions. As people walked by wondering why this mom had steam coming out of her ears, I politely smiled and nodded as she piled on a tirade of criticism. Fortunately at that moment, one of my volunteer moms (who knew our plans very well) was walking by. I was able to stop her and ask if she could help me explain where I was coming from. I acknowledge that I probably hadn't done a good job explaining things and needed her help. Not only was it a great day to have a parent volunteer on my team, it was also a great day for an irate parent to see that we were all on the same team together. Seeing the decision through the lens of another parent made all the difference, and it taught me the importance of having parents who would one day be advocates for me.

We gain perspective. Just being able to sit down with parents and talk through ministry plans has given me great insights into their world. Not long ago I looked to make a change to the night of the week our high school large group was meeting on. Prior to the decision, we surveyed as many parents as possible and recruited a small team of parents to help dissect the findings. Even though the survey concluded a need to change, my parent team helped me see some of the tensions such a change would bring to certain families. By understanding these tensions, we were able to construct a good communication plan that addressed them ahead of time. Having parents' perspectives on this issue allowed us to defuse potential conflicts and allowed other parents to see that we had considered their thoughts and feelings. I would never have seen those tensions on my own.

Partnering with parents begins with getting on the same team with them. But it doesn't stop there. As you develop an understanding of their needs and the strengths they bring to the team, you'll build a team that can work together to do some great things.

GAME PLAN SUMMARY

The way we view parents affects the partnerships we develop with them. Viewing parents as being on the same team leads to greater effectiveness in reaching and equipping the next generation for Christ.

TEAM UP!

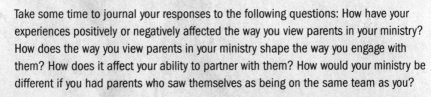

PRACTICE DRILLS

*Use the following action steps to help you apply
what you've learned to your life and ministry.*

1. Take some time to journal your responses to the following questions: How have your experiences positively or negatively affected the way you view parents in your ministry? How does the way you view parents in your ministry shape the way you engage with them? How does it affect your ability to partner with them? How would your ministry be different if you had parents who saw themselves as being on the same team as you?

2. Divide a sheet of paper into three columns. In the first column, create a list of difficult parents in your ministry. In the second column, list any fears or struggles you're aware of that each of those parents is facing. In the third column, write down some ways you could encourage those parents regarding their fears and struggles. Take time to pray for each of the parents on your list, and ask God to give you wisdom in how to come alongside those parents.

3. List some of the places you most often see parents. For each of those places, identify one step you can take to free yourself up to listen to the parents you see in those places. If any of those steps require advanced planning on your part (such as having an adult volunteer who is able to take over with kids while you interact with parents), begin making those arrangements today.

4. Contact three or four key parents, and ask them to be your eyes and ears in ministry. Meet with those parents, presenting a basic agenda of decisions they could help you think through and focusing on asking them questions rather than casting a vision. Aside from questions about specific decisions you're working through, ask questions such as:

   - What are the major issues our parents are struggling with as they raise their kids in the faith?
   - What would our parents want me to know about them or their kids but are too afraid to share?
   - How approachable am I to parents?
   - What are we doing to help parents instill faith at home? What could we do better?

5. Take 15 minutes to pray for your parents today. Ask God to bring to mind those parents who could be struggling. Take another 15 minutes to send a note, a text, or an email to encourage those parents and let them know you're praying for them.

Chapter 4

CAST THE
BIBLICAL VISION

*The importance of helping parents
and church leadership see the biblical
case for partnering with parents.*

I grew up outside the church. My parents and I only went to church for weddings and funerals. In fact, the first time I went to a church on my own was when my friend and I decided to break in to steal some candy from the youth group candy stash. God has an incredible sense of humor since, just a year later, I was invited by a friend to attend that same youth group. Even though I thought I might be struck by lightning when I set foot back in that church, I said yes. From there I spent the next four years hearing about Christ and seeing an incredible example of God-honoring leaders who showed great patience with me. At the age of 18, I accepted Christ and my life was forever changed.

Fast forward many years. I was married to Lisa. I was in full-time ministry. We had a mortgage and the first of our three children. There I was, a pastor in a local church who had absolutely no idea how to raise my kids in their faith journey. No one had ever shown me what to do or what to say. Talking about faith was absolutely foreign to my parents. As a new father to little Emma, I desperately searched for advice, wisdom, and some keys to raising my kids with a solid faith foundation. I knew it was my job to invest in my kids first, but getting started was a lot harder than I anticipated. Over the years I've come to realize that I'm not the only parent who's had similar feelings of inadequacy. I've also come to see that many parents have gone before me and made an eternal difference in the lives of their kids.

We Need to Capture the Vision

Most parents I meet don't know where to begin either when it comes to raising their kids with a solid faith foundation. In fact, many parents I meet don't even realize it's their God-given role to invest in their children's faith journey. This problem is amplified by the unspoken expectation many parents have that it's the children's pastor's role to equip their kids for a lifelong faith journey. Even if parents do know that it's their role to invest in their kids, many of them are often so overwhelmed with their work and extracurricular family activities that they don't make time to invest in their kids. These are the parents I struggle with the most. They know their role, but they choose to make sports, academics, and personal fulfillment a greater priority than their child's faith journey.

Before we get parents on board with a vision for raising their kids in the faith, it's important that we understand what the Bible says about the part we play in pursuing that vision. If all we do is point fingers at parents, we're missing the big picture. We all have a role to play in accomplishing God's purposes for the children and students he's entrusted to us.

Deuteronomy 6:4-9 says:

"Listen, O Israel! The Lord is our God, the Lord alone. And you must love the Lord your God with all your heart, all your soul, and all your strength. And you must commit yourselves whole-heartedly to these commands that I am giving you today. Repeat them again and again to your children. Talk about them when you are at home and when you are on the road, when you are going to bed and when you are getting up. Tie them to your hands and wear them on your forehead as reminders. Write them on the doorposts of your house and on your gates."

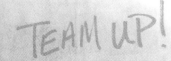

Picture this incredible and historic moment with me for a moment. After 40 years of wandering in a desert due to unbelief and complaining, Moses and his people arrived at a destination that should have only taken 11 days to find (Deuteronomy 1:2). You can imagine their relief and expectation as they stood there on the plains of Moab, sensing this was a new beginning for a whole generation of people. The atmosphere of change was in the air, and their waiting and wandering in the desert had finally come to an end. Imagine the faces of the people as they stood before Moses and waited for him to speak. This was it. This was the beginning of a new movement, a new chapter, and a new destination. The people were ready to hear from their leader, and they were ready to go the next mile in discovering God's new blessing. They were ready to take new ground and move beyond the failures of the previous generation. As Moses began to speak, they were hanging on every word, every instruction, and every command. What they heard would be groundbreaking and would guide their whole nation for generations to come.

It's critical that we understand the importance of Moses' words to his people at that time. It's also essential we understand the importance of those words to us today. That's what the rest of this chapter is about. Moses' words are relevant to you and me as we look to improve upon the past and forge ahead in influencing the world for Christ. Much is at stake in reaching and equipping the next generation for Christ.

Looking back over the past few decades, we can see that the lack of synchronization in our churches regarding our approach to children's and student ministries—along with a consumer mentality—has caused us to lose sight of a biblical vision for reaching the next generation. Many leaders in the church have fostered a "leave it to the experts" mentality (albeit unconsciously at times), and many parents have played along with it. Let me give you an example.

Emily's parents understand the cost of having a child play on a traveling sports team, but they also see how well Emily is developing as a soccer player. Her soccer coach, Drew, is a great inspiration. He clearly loves the sport and has a great pedigree, having played collegiate soccer and won numerous titles at the semi-professional level. As for school, Emily's parents couldn't be happier with the teachers who invest in her academics each day. Moving to a new house and changing to one of the state's premier school systems was well worth it. So much has changed in the past decade that it's hard to keep up with what Emily is learning today. And between Emily's soccer schedule, youth group activities, and her parents' careers, there's little time for them to keep up with all the academic changes.

Emily's parents are thankful to have a network of support for Emily as she navigates adolescence and looks forward to college. They're especially thankful for the church they've been attending. They love being part of a church where their kids are loved and receive engaging teaching that's relevant to them. Now that Emily is in middle school and becoming more autonomous and more aware of a fast-changing culture, her parents are particularly thankful for Emily's youth pastor. In their eyes, he understands teenagers so much better than they do and seems to have a greater connection with them. Emily's parents see that he knows the Bible better than they do, too, and knows how to explain things to Emily in ways she connects with. Even when Emily attended children's church, her parents thought the leaders there just had a better way of engaging with and speaking to the kids about Jesus than they ever could. The children's workers just knew what to say and what to do.

Does that sound familiar? Emily's parents are typical of many parents you and I meet every day. They're busy and stretched and looking for "experts" to come alongside them as they raise their kids. While this makes sense in some areas, God never intended parents to leave their child's faith development to someone else. Sadly though, many of us in church leadership have often affirmed this approach by creating silo programs that are solely focused on children and students with little to no consideration for parents—either in terms of how we can equip them or how we can involve them. It's as if we've said, "Leave it to us, we'll teach your kids what they need to know. Give us an hour a week, and we've got you covered."

Now I don't think most pastors intentionally communicate that parents are unimportant or mean to leave them out of the picture, but our modern-day church culture has often caused it to happen. In addition to pushing parents to the sidelines, it's also created an impossible task for children's and youth pastors to accomplish. And for those parents who are intent on investing in their child's faith journey, they feel alone as they look to the church for help.

TEAM UP!

We Need to Understand the Vision

God's vision and design for raising the next generation is for it to be done as a partnership between parents and the church. It's time that we come back to that vision and design; the one that Moses gave his people many centuries ago. As we look back at some of the failures of the past, it's essential that you and I take new ground as we partner with parents in raising their kids in a solid faith foundation. To do that, let's look more closely at those great words Moses spoke to the waiting generation in his day. Let's take those words and build a bridge of application to our world today.

It's for Everyone

"Listen, O Israel!" (Deuteronomy 6:4)

For years I had missed the importance of those three words in the context of this passage. As a pastor who works with families, my default has always been to focus on the role that parents play in impressing God's commands on their children. It's the part I want parents to get. It's the part that allows me to emphasize their role and take the responsibility off of my shoulders. However, that only works if I ignore those first three words. You see, when Moses gave this command it was for a whole nation and people, not just one targeted segment. Its central message wasn't just for parents, and it wasn't just for the church. It was a message for the whole faith community to commit to and to live out for generations to come. And the same is true for us today. Reaching and equipping the next generation for Christ depends on everyone in our faith communities. That includes parents, you, other church leaders, the college grad who just moved back home, the empty-nester couple who now love to travel, and even the church janitor who doesn't particularly like kids. Everyone has a part to play.

An old proverb says that it takes a village to raise a child. In our world today that idea is quickly becoming distant, consumer driven, and shallow; the village mindset is being lost. No one seems to want to take responsibility. It's always someone else's job to take care of the kids.

As leaders in the church, part of our role is to cast the vision that, when it comes to reaching children and students, we're all in this together.

It's a responsibility for the whole church to take on. It's a call to ensure that everyone (even your church janitor) understands that they have a role to play in reaching and equipping the next generation for Christ. "Listen, O Israel" was for a whole people group, and it's for your whole church to grasp on to today.

In our church, baptisms or dedications are oftentimes when the pastor charges the congregation to support parents as they commit to raise their children in the Christian faith. During such ceremonies, the pastor asks the congregation to commit to supporting the child and his or her parents, at which time everyone stands up and declares, "We will by the grace of God." However, it's possible for people to forget what they just agreed to as soon as they sit back down. Therefore, it's important that we continue to cast the vision for a "village" mindset whenever we can. We can't just talk about it at baptisms or dedications and hope that it'll stick.

It Begins With Me

> "And you must love the Lord your God with all your heart, all your soul, and all your strength. And you must commit yourselves wholeheartedly to these commands that I am giving you today" (Deuteronomy 6:5-6).

Just as we discussed in an earlier chapter, it's crucial that God's commandments be written on our own hearts first so that we can be a light to those we lead. Perhaps the most powerful advice I was ever given by a mentor was to ensure, first and foremost, that my own faith walk was strong and authentic. If God's truth is impressed on my own heart, it will authenticate all that I teach and train in my own household. That's why I've also told parents the best gift they can give their children is an authentic faith that shows a love for God and for others. It's vital that you and I encourage parents to grow in their faith and promote other ministries in the church that will be a support to parents. For example, even though I don't oversee small groups in my church, I'm constantly talking about and promoting them to the parents I meet. When parents are growing in their faith through small groups, I know that'll have an effect on the teaching their kids will receive at home.

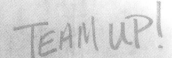

It's Ongoing

"Repeat them again and again to your children. Talk about them when you are at home and when you are on the road, when you are going to bed and when you are getting up. Tie them to your hands and wear them on your forehead as reminders. Write them on the doorposts of your house and on your gates" (Deuteronomy 6:7-9).

One of the challenges parents face is how to communicate God's truth to their children. I've read a lot of books for parents that have lofty ideas and present wildly complex systems for instilling faith in my children. I often walk away from them feeling overwhelmed or confused as to where and how to begin. That's where Moses' words can help parents see that passing on the faith to their children doesn't have to be rocket science. It's simply about grabbing on to the teachable times and creating intentional moments with our children. (I'll explain more of what I mean by that later.) It's the same thing Jesus did with his disciples. Some of their greatest lessons came as they walked and talked and engaged in life together. That's great news for parents and for us.

As we communicate to parents the vision for passing on the faith to their kids, it's important that we distance ourselves from lofty, ambiguous ideas and offer them practical and specific ways to accomplish the task. After all, it's the practical and specific that parents will be most likely to implement.

There are natural and normal opportunities that parents have to introduce faith into conversations with their kids. By taking advantage of those opportunities, parents can create a culture in their homes of having faith talks throughout the day. Over time such talks become natural and normal for both kids and parents and feel less forced. Deuteronomy 6:7-9 outlines some of those opportunities for us. *The Apologetics Study Bible* sums it up like this: "By means of a figure of speech Moses uses opposites—sitting and walking, lying down and rising up—to suggest that any time is appropriate for instruction in the ways of the Lord." While it seems that Moses didn't mean for those times to be taken literally, I've found that they create an outline of sorts that can be useful for parents as they consider how to invest in their children. Let's take a look at each of those times now.

When you're at home. Even the busiest family will have times they're all gathered around a table for a meal. Granted, as kids get older and extracurricular activities are in full force, having time together around the dinner table gets harder to come by. But when you do find the time, it's a great opportunity to thank God together for his blessings and debrief the day, acknowledging things God has done.

When you're on the road. Growing up in England, I remember times walking down the road with my mom or dad as we went to a friend's house or to the soccer field. However, here in the States my experience has been that there are fewer sidewalks and everything's far away (at least by English standards). So I apply this idea to my time in the car with my kids—no matter how short a distance we travel. My oldest daughter's previous school was about one mile from our house, so we could literally walk along the road. However, if you know my poky little girl, you understand that getting going in the morning has always been a challenge, and a car ride was usually needed. Even on the short journey to school each morning, we shared prayer requests for the day and prayed for each other. And at the end of day when I picked her up, it was always a great time to debrief her highs and lows and talk about what God might have been teaching her during the day.

When you're going to bed and when you're getting up. Right from our eldest child's birth, Lisa and I created a habit of reading the Bible and praying with our kids before bed. There are some days we do better at it than others, but those times have become part of our family's culture that are hard to miss or forget. Recently after a long day out and returning home late, I decided to cut out our Bible time and simply pray with my two girls. Oh my goodness! You would have thought I had grounded them both for two weeks. They created such a stir and gave me such a guilt trip for not reading together that I had to give in.

Here's the brilliant thing about encouraging parents to take those teachable moments at bedtime: For the most part, children (students included) just seem to be more spiritually sensitive and a lot more open at bedtime. It's almost like the Holy Spirit has softened them up and helped them to tune in to him in greater ways. Just a few weeks ago as I was kissing my 5-year-old good night, she asked, "Daddy, if God loves all people, why does he allow some people to go to hell?" In the busyness of the day, it's possible that kind

of question would have never even been asked (or answered). But as the day was winding down and my daughter was settling in for bed, her heart opened up—as did a great opportunity to speak into her life.

I used to think that passing on the faith would require me to implement lofty ideas with a great deal of planning and struggle. Sadly, many parents I meet have a similar view on what's required of them. They either try too hard, implement something their kids dislike (some might use the word "hate"), or give up altogether. Just before the birth of my eldest child, I sought advice from parents whose kids were older and who I thought had done a good job passing on the faith. One parent I spoke to named Deb shared some wisdom that immediately alleviated my fears and gave me instant confidence that I could make a difference. She said:

> "First of all, it's by the grace of God that he used me. And second, it's all about the teachable times and bringing faith into everyday situations, times, and places."

If you have kids of your own, take Deb's advice and use the teachable moments to make faith stick with your kids. Encourage the parents in your ministry to do the same. Her counsel is simple, yet powerful. I've experienced the benefit of creating teachable times in my own household with my kids. You and the parents to whom you minister can do the same.

It's Intentional

> "Tie them to your hands and wear them on your forehead as reminders. Write them on the doorposts of your house and on your gates" (Deuteronomy 6:8-9).

Throughout the centuries, Jewish families have taken these verses quite literally. According to *The Teacher's Bible Commentary,* they tied small boxes containing words from the Torah to their hands and foreheads and also placed copies of the Torah on their doorposts. But many commentators would agree that Moses didn't intend these verses to be applied in this way. Rather, he was communicating the principle of creating intentional traditions, monuments, or milestones that would keep God's truth at the forefront of families' priorities. Such practices become reminders of God's grace in the life of a child as well as a road map of growth for a family to follow. In the chapter on milestones, we'll look at how to do these things more specifically. But perhaps the most important thing for parents to understand is that creating intentional moments, traditions, and experiences gives their children goals to look forward to and markers to look back on as they grow. By helping parents understand this, we encourage them to integrate a culture of faith into their family's lives rather than separating faith from everyday living.

We Need to Cast the Vision

Influencing church leadership to embrace a vision of reaching the whole family is critical. After all, your leaders set the direction of the church. And if a church employs you, it's likely you'll have to get them to buy into partnering with parents. But that's not always easy to do.

In a previous church, a senior leader promised me that he was committed to reaching parents just as much as reaching their kids. However, after being there for a year, I saw clearly that what mattered was producing a knockout youth ministry program that would bring more families to the church. The idea of expending energy to partner with parents was foreign and was seen as a drain on creating an incredible youth ministry. It certainly wasn't written in my job description. And in hindsight I wish I'd done more in the interview process to ensure that partnering with parents was a priority. However, despite this disparity in vision, it didn't prevent me from finding ways to cast the vision to those over me and build consensus about partnering with parents.

Influencing our senior leaders is a slow process and takes a lot of work, but it's essential if we're going to successfully incorporate partnering with parents into our ministries. Let's finish out this chapter by taking a look at some healthy ways to go about it.

Focus on your job description first. It doesn't matter if you're a volunteer or paid staff, the leaders in your church see your primary responsibility as investing in children or students (or both). We have to remember that the idea of partnering with parents and the titles of "Next Generation Pastor" or "Family Life Pastor" are foreign to many leaders in the church. We also have to consider that there's a certain way

 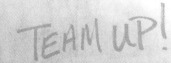

children's and youth ministry has been done over the years. Therefore, it's essential that we gain influence first by doing a great job in the roles we were hired to fill. In previous churches it has taken me nearly two years to establish a ministry that gave me the credibility to add in a greater focus on partnering with parents. However, that didn't mean I couldn't lay groundwork as I went.

Pursue the healthy conversations. Part of our role is to constantly find ways to passionately communicate to those who lead us the need and vision to partner with parents. However, in my experience it's crucial to pursue such conversations in ways that are positive and that advocate the reasons for partnering with parents, as opposed to criticizing what the church is missing out on. In pursuing healthy conversations with the decision-makers in your church, keep in mind that they're usually managing multiple people, plans, and ideas. So ensure that you come prepared, and give it time.

Own the vision. When you own the vision yourself, you'll be able to communicate it not just out of your head, but from your heart. And that'll greatly increase your ability to persuade those above you. But owning the vision means more than just being passionate. It means being thoughtful as well. Learn to articulate why it's essential to partner with parents in a sentence or two. Provide a biblical basis along with some practical examples of how partnering with parents is more effective. Take the vision and begin formulating it into a plan. If you don't feel ready to do those things yet, I hope that by the end of this book you'll have found some good ideas to get started with.

Have a strategy. One of the greatest shortcomings in my early days was not having a good strategy that other leaders could support. While many were quick to agree with the idea of partnering with parents, none of them had really ever thought through what that truly meant. For many of them, it seemed like we were already partnering with parents. Communicating a strategy that includes a timeline and specific steps showing a progression of implementation is crucial. But continue to work on meeting the goals your senior leader has set for you as well. Even if you have a good strategy, they're ultimately going to measure your success by the program you develop for kids.

Share stories. A story of life change is always going to be the most effective way to cast vision with leaders in the local church. We all want to know one thing: Does it work? Providing stories of how partnering with parents is making your ministry more effective and how it's helping parents to be more effective is crucial. We recently created an event for parents and children to celebrate and serve together over Christmas. The event itself was nothing out of this world, but it was a great way to help parents and children focus outwardly during the Christmas season. Following the event, we posted a number of photos of kids and parents serving together, and we even created a quick video to show at our Christmas Eve services. (Be sure to get parents' permission ahead of time whenever you picture kids.) The following week there were countless responses to the photos from proud parents who thanked us for the opportunity to serve with their children. Being able to cast vision with key leaders through the comments of those parents was simple, but effective.

Request stage time in big church. I'm very fortunate in my present church when it comes to my senior pastor and executive director supporting the vision to partner with parents. It's not difficult to ask for opportunities to cast the vision to the entire church. However, that's not always been the case in the previous churches I've worked in.

Even though there are always many events to be promoted and that require stage time, it doesn't mean we can't ask for it, too. As long as you don't come across as a whiny kid, you might be surprised at the opportunities that come your way. That being said, if your church just isn't able to give you stage time, don't worry. Having been in a church that didn't have space in the schedule for time like this, I can tell you that it's not absolutely essential. Helpful, yes. Essential, no.

Commit to the long haul. One of the greatest ways to help your leadership capture the vision for partnering with parents is longevity. The longer you stay, the greater your influence. In my experience, it usually takes about two years to establish relationships, figure out how things work, and develop a track record to point to before you have the clout to recommend changes to what's expected of you. Depending on the culture of your church and the leaders who make the decisions, it'll take time to make progress toward partnering with parents. Perhaps the most effective step you can take in

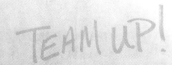
TEAM UP!

that direction is to get to know the influential leaders in your church and give them the opportunity to get to know and trust you.

So many leaders have an unrealistic outlook on what it takes to cast vision and bring change in a church. They seem surprised when people aren't fully on board with their new vision and incredibly innovative ideas. It's not that the vision is off or that the ideas aren't solid. It's often a matter of too fast, too soon. The ability to influence others—especially those over you—comes by forming trusting relationships, and such relationships are developed over the long haul.

GAME PLAN SUMMARY

In a world of competing priorities, parents need a biblical, compelling, and practical vision for reaching and equipping their children in the faith.

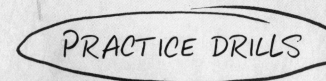

PRACTICE DRILLS

*Use the following action steps to help you apply
what you've learned to your life and ministry.*

1. Identify one or two Bible passages that support your vision to reach the next generation through partnering with parents. Take time to reflect on those passages, writing down any insights you find. Take time to pray, asking God to help you know how to use those insights to cast the vision of partnering with parents to others.

2. Contact three or four key leaders in your church who could help you cast vision and influence others with the vision to partner with parents. Set up a time with each of those leaders to share your heart and cast the vision.

3. Give copies of this book to influential leaders in your church, and ask them to read it. Tell them you'd like to hear their thoughts about the ideas it contains, and set up a time to meet with them and discuss those ideas.

4. Identify ways outside of formal meetings in which you can continuously cast vision to parents, volunteers, and church leaders. How can you weave the vision for partnering with parents into your regular communication pieces? Where could you go that would provide you the opportunity to interact with the people you want to catch this vision? How do you demonstrate the vision of partnering with parents in the way you interact with the people in your church?

TEAM UP!

Chapter 5

COMMUNICATE STRATEGICALLY

*Ideas for helping parents
hear you over the noise.*

The event you've been preparing for months is nearly ready to kick off. With the focus on kids and parents coming together to celebrate and serve, this could be a game changer for your church. There's no end to the opportunities for you and your numerous volunteers to connect with parents, not to mention the relationships that'll be built between the parents. The auditorium has been decorated by you and a hardworking team of volunteers. Everyone's in place. There's an air of excitement and expectation as your team gets ready to see the excited faces of kids and parents as they come through the doors.

Fast forward an hour. Parents and kids are present in body, though not necessarily in spirit. You survey the large room, keenly aware that you and your team nearly outnumber the group of participants. Inside you feel far from celebrating, but your feelings aren't immediately noticeable to those around you. As you look around the room at your team of volunteers, their faces display a look of forced excitement at best, deflation at worst, and an unspoken question: Where is everyone?

The drive home is filled with more questions as you reflect on the event and the lack of participation. The conversation in your head goes something like this:

"Really? Why didn't they show up? Don't they care about their kids? This was in the church bulletin for four weeks. We even sent home a flier with all of their kids. What's the point of partnering with parents if they don't want to partner back? Sometimes I think I care more about their kids than they do!"

At the stoplight you're ranting angrily to yourself and at God as you find yourself utterly deflated. For a moment you find some levity as you catch a glimpse of the person in the car next to you staring inside your car looking for the person you're spewing to. But alas, they conclude you're crazy and drive away quickly. You conclude that you might be as well, and that it's the parents who are the cause of your craziness.

Parents Are on Information Overload

Does this situation sound familiar? I can't tell you how many times I've put my heart and soul into an event only to have a dismal turnout. Unfortunately, this is par for the course in ministry. But it's a course that doesn't have to be repeated with great frequency. Whether it's an event for kids, for their parents, or both, it's imperative that you and I realize that we live in a world where parents are bombarded by hundreds, if not thousands, of messages every week. It's a phenomenon I call "promotion dilution." I don't know if anyone has coined that phrase before, but it's one that I use a lot in my ministry. So if you've never heard it before, you can say you heard it first from some British guy.

Promotion dilution occurs when our churches attempt to promote too many events and programs at a given time. In our charge to promote everything we're doing, nothing really gets highlighted. Instead the message behind every event and program is watered down as it competes with all of the other events and programs we offer. The fact is that people tend to gravitate to what's promoted the most and talked about with the greatest focus. All of this is why, in my present church, we've learned to become strategic with elevating certain programs and events into the view of the congregation.

Consider how much promotion dilution is occurring for the parents of the kids and students you're trying to reach. They live in a world of constant communication as individuals, companies, schools, and churches vie for

 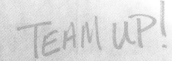

their attention and participation. Your church is one of thousands of competing voices. I only have to look at my own life to see how this plays out.

First there's the plethora of paperwork my kids bring home from school. Then there's the junk mail from companies offering deals that seem too good to be true. On top of that, my inbox is jam-packed with emails from teachers, school superintendents, and our favorite stores offering "the best deal ever." And that's just my personal email account! I currently have over 4,000 unopened emails that, at one time, I set aside to read later. (Most of these are promotional emails, but if yours is one of them…sorry about that.) Social media doesn't help either. These days I seem to miss half the updates from friends and family. I got to the point where I had to turn off the notifications on my phone. Speaking of phones, mine is in silent mode on a regular basis. Every evening I get calls from telemarketers or some recorded political call.

I could go on and on. We live a fast-moving world where communication is constant. And by the time this book is in your hands, there's likely to be some new communication device that makes it even faster.

If you took a moment to consider just how much information and promotion comes your way on a weekly basis, you might just blow a gasket! And the same is probably true for most of the parents you communicate with. We've already established that parents are harassed and harried; now add in the thousands of messages competing for their attention and participation. You're one of thousands of other voices vying for the attention and participation of parents in a world of promotion dilution. It's naïve to expect parents to get your message quickly.

Whether or not your church has a formal bulletin that's handed out as people come into your building on Sunday, it's likely that you have a particular place in your church that's the primary distribution point for getting information to your church family. But even if parents do read the church bulletin on Sunday morning, they've likely forgotten what they read and have misplaced the bulletin (or just threw it out) by the time Monday rolls around. What's more, sickness, sporting events, and family getaways mean that typical attendance is about twice a month for a lot of families. Therefore, they only get to see your information about twice a month (and that's assuming they read the bulletin).

We have to accept that we live in a world in which parents receive constant communication from a multitude of sources. Whether it's the local school, the sports coach, a corporation, or some shady guy in another country, you and I are in competition for the attention of the parents we're trying to reach. And the competition is stiff. So what are we to do?

Say Things Multiple Times in Multiple Ways

Even though we have stiff competition for the attention of parents and kids, there are some ways that we can engage them and assist them in making faith a greater priority. We can learn a great deal from the research and techniques that marketing companies are already employing while also leveraging our unique identity as the church to get an open door to a parent's focus and commitment.

In the world of sales and business, experts maintain that it requires many "touches" with a single person before that person buys a product. That means a salesperson or business has to connect with and present information to people several times before those people become customers or clients. While we're not salespeople, we have to accept that we live in a consumer-driven world where the goal is to get a person to buy into a product or service. Our brains have been trained to tune in to a consumer-driven world in the way we engage with media and marketing. While the church isn't merely a product or service, it's still imperative that we recognize how people's brains are wired and how they'll process and respond to the information we send them. That means we'll have to communicate to parents with multiple touches as well. We might not like this reality, but it's very unlikely that the average parent will get your message the first time around.

In my ministry we use a messaging service that tracks exactly who has opened a message and how many have opened it. It's sometimes amusing to speak to that one parent who claims to have never seen a particular email, yet I can clearly see that it was opened. I've also come to realize that I'm that parent at times. A quick look at a message on my phone, and I've soon forgotten that I even saw it, much less whether I replied to it. It's as if the message was invisible. All that has helped me realize that an effective message needs to be in front of someone several times before they really "see" it.

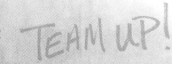

Perhaps one of the most startling statistics I've discovered is that about 40 to 50 percent of the parents in my church will never open my messages at all. Our church is doing far better than the industry average of 25.76 percent for a nonprofit (this according to MailChimp Research). It's still unsettling that many parents will never even give our messages the time of day, but that's the reality we have to face.

While communicating a message with multiple touches is necessary, it's also imperative that we communicate in multiple modes. With the onset of social media, I used to hear that many companies were likely to abandon other "outdated" modes of communicating with their potential customers. However, as I survey the landscape of sales and media, I see that companies are still using multiple avenues to communicate with their potential customer base.

Recently a popular car manufacturer showed up in my social media feed offering me the chance to win one of its incredible cars. Since I'm in full-time ministry and have the junkiest minivan on planet Earth, I saw this as my only viable opportunity to own a brand-new car with all the bells and whistles on it. Without hesitation I gave them all the information they asked for, and I even entered my wife's name, too. (She wasn't impressed.) In the last few months we've both received multiple emails from this car company along with glossy brochures in the mail. I regularly see this company show up on my social media feed along with the commercials I come across on TV and the radio. (Yes, I'm one of those people who still listens to the radio.) The point in all of this is that not only has this company communicated to me multiple times, but it has also communicated to me in multiple ways.

Not all parents are wired the same when it comes to communication. Some don't particularly care for technology or use it well, preferring instead to talk in person or receive a physical mailing. Others don't care for printed postcards, letters, or even phone calls, opting for email or text messages. A number of years ago I came to realize that I was expecting parents to want to communicate in the way I preferred. Rather than promoting things through a variety of means, I was gravitating to what I liked best. In the process, I was narrowing my audience reach and missing out on getting pertinent information into the hands of parents. If we want to have parents commit to our events and programs, it's crucial that we accept the need to get beyond our own preferences and communicate in multiple modes and at multiple times.

Manage the Frequency of Your Communication

"Is there a possibility of overcommunicating with parents? Will they tune you out if you send them too many messages?" This is a valid question a friend who is serving in another ministry asked me recently. His concern is well-founded in our world of promotion dilution. Simply stated, there's a balance to be found. Just as multiple focuses can easily lead to promotion dilution, it doesn't take much for parents to feel as if they've heard your message so many times they can ignore the communications you send them in the future. Worse yet is the possibility of them feeling like you're harassing them, which you definitely don't want. While multiple modes and multiple messages are essential, it also takes strategic management of the frequency with which we communicate.

I wish I could tell you that managing your communication is an exact science, but I've found that every community and church culture responds differently to the frequency of communication. Right now I live in a fast-paced community that's full of high-achieving parents whose kids are following in their parents' footsteps. In this context I can get away with a greater frequency of communication compared to other places I've served. Perhaps the most helpful piece of advice I can give you on this is to just ask the parents. In my ministry I have three or four go-to parents whom I trust to give me honest feedback. Find some parents in your ministry who can give you honest feedback as well, and ask them to evaluate whether you need to adjust the frequency of your communication and in what way.

Given that people move to new houses and change email addresses and cellphone numbers, it's possible that you don't have current information for contacting parents. In my context every new family registration and every event is an opportunity to gather information from parents and ask their permission to communicate with them. (Asking parents for permission is critical. It helps gain both buy in and trust from the parents and shows them you're taking them into consideration.)

 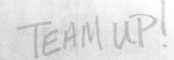

Last summer we had two large events back to back that allowed us to engage with a massive number of parents—a weeklong camp held at our church and an all-church picnic. We already communicated regularly with some of the parents, and there were some who only knew about us through the church bulletin. (I guess it does work sometimes.) At both of these events, we offered cards for families to fill out and enter to win some brilliant prizes. From these two events we were able to add numerous families to our regular communications lists.

No matter what your context is, it's important to space out your communications appropriately. It makes them feel less annoying and more helpful to parents. Here's an example of how I try to space out communications in my ministry:

Regular communications
- Twice-yearly letters to all parents
- Quarterly calendars of upcoming and notable events
- Monthly emailed newsletters or ministry overviews
- Weekly text message updates and reminders (linked to social media)
- Weekly social media updates
- Weekly parent take-homes for children's ministry

Special event promotions
- Postcards mailed three to four weeks ahead of a special event
- A short promotional video three to four weeks ahead of the event posted on social media
- Weekly social media updates starting two to three weeks ahead of the event
- Weekly email updates two to three weeks ahead of an event (spaced a couple of days apart from social media updates)
- Information included in our monthly parent newsletter
- Postcards sent home with children/students one to two weeks before the event
- Text message reminders sent the week of the event

"Seriously? You do all that?" you ask. Yes…and no. That's the ideal for our ministry. And it is what we're doing for an event that we're currently working toward. However, we're not actually a church that has the resources to pull together a massive marketing campaign like that on a regular basis.

If you're creating an event that's appealing to parents and their kids, it's far more likely that you'll have greater success with attendance if you increase the time and resources you give to promotion ahead of the event. While I can't guarantee you'll need to expand your church facilities to accommodate a huge turnout, my experience has shown me that promotion through multiple communication modes over multiple times with a strategic schedule always beats a bulletin announcement and an email. While it takes a lot of work and intentional planning, I'm convinced it's well worth it.

Build Relationships With Parents

I wish I could say that was it, but there are some even more essential components that are worth reminding you of and pointing you to. So before we continue, take a deep breath and remember that you don't have to implement everything all at once. Be thinking about how you can weave one or two ideas into what you're already doing.

While the world of marketing has moved toward a repetitive, diversified, and strategic plan, it also understands the importance of relationship. It's the game changer when it comes to getting your message across. Good communication allows us to knock on the doors of parents; it's relationship that lets us in. When personal relationships with the families you work with are combined with multiple touches and multiple modes of communication that are managed strategically, your voice will begin to stand out. Your ability to get parents to show up to that incredible event or for them to make your children's ministry program the highlight of their child's week is deeply tied to relationships.

Relational investment builds trust and influence with parents. Parents will give their time and resources to leaders in the church they know and trust. Your relationship with parents is the greatest way to build a bridge to them owning and participating in the vision to reach and equip the next generation. It does take some time and requires a long-term view, but it can also lead parents to a long-term commitment to partnering with you in investing in their child's faith journey.

A common statement in children's and youth ministry circles is, "I know I need to partner with parents, but I'm so busy doing ministry with

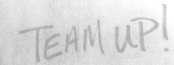

their kids that I don't have time to build relationships with them, too." Not long ago I had someone say to me, "You're a family ministry guy now; of course you have time to partner with parents." But in reality I've been building relationships with parents long before I took the role as a family pastor/next generation pastor. Doing it really doesn't require spending a lot of extra time. One brief, caring conversation at a time is all it takes.

How to Increase Your Face Time With Parents

When a parent can look you in the eye or hear your voice on the phone, it's more likely he or she will give your ministry greater focus and commitment. Let's take a look at some ways to better get in front of parents and build relationships with them.

Find time and make time. Take a look at when the parents in your ministry are naturally and normally around. For many of us, Sunday morning presents the greatest opportunity to meet and get to know parents. For others it might be at a midweek program. In the last 15 years, I've made it my goal to free myself up as much as possible on Sunday mornings and at the end of midweek events so I can meet

THE BENEFITS OF INVESTING IN RELATIONSHIPS

In a world of sleek promotion and bottom-line sales goals, there's a great shortage of people who genuinely care these days. Even many of our schoolteachers and coaches have become too focused on test scores or securing wins to the detriment of genuinely caring for kids and parents. We live in a world that's so focused on results that it neglects the need for relationships. When you and I take time to invest in relationships and have caring conversations with parents, we stand out from the noisy and impersonal crowd. Consider these other benefits:

- When you take time to talk face to face with parents about how to engage their child in simple faith conversations at home, you're investing in that child's faith journey.

- A personal invitation to an activity or event through a phone call or hand-written note can have a much greater effect than an impersonal email.

- Emails can be made to feel more personal with a quick in-person connection ahead of time.

- One or two conversations per week with parents can add up to greater overall engagement and commitment through the course of a year.

- When you create space in your schedule for face-to-face time with parents, they'll be more willing to create space on their calendars for ministry events and programs.

and connect with parents of the kids and students I'm ministering to. In fact, on any given Sunday morning it would be easy for anyone watching me to accuse me of being lazy and not having anything to do. I spend a lot of time standing around the lobby and hallways drinking coffee and engaging with parents. Sounds like a great job, doesn't it? However, this is completely intentional on my part. It gives me the opportunity to have strategic conversations with the parents of kids I'm trying to reach and equip.

Whether you're paid staff or a volunteer, it's essential that you find ways to free yourself up and make time to talk to parents. Allowing ourselves to get overly consumed with ministering directly to kids can often mean we're unavailable to engage in meaningful conversations with parents. If that describes you, consider how you could delegate a responsibility to free yourself up to engage more with parents.

Divide your time. Most of us are employed by or volunteer at churches that prioritize investing directly in kids' lives. And frankly, that's what we want to be doing as well. The idea of using our time to talk to parents as we watch kids arrive and allow them to pass by creates tension for us at times. It also has the potential for creating tension in others. Those who don't understand the importance of partnering with parents might think we're giving up vital opportunities to invest in kids as we stand around and talk with their parents.

Practically speaking, though, I've had to make the choice to seek out two or three parents each week to talk to and encourage, knowing that in some way I'll feel like I'm missing out on contact time with kids. What helps is having a broad view of my ministry. It allows me to be confident that my investment in parents is an investment in the whole family. That's a view that all of us need to have. Yes, it's still important that we invest in the kids. But it's imperative that we give time to their parents as well. If you're in a large church environment, consider what the effect would be if other staff members and volunteers were to each choose one parent to talk to and encourage each week. Imagine what the consequences of those conversations might be a year or two from now. Think about the significance they could have at home for the kids.

Consolidate your efforts. If you're able to get out to watch one of the kids in your ministry in something like a play or a sporting event, consider

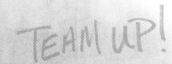

how you can use it as an opportunity to talk to parents, too. When I go to visit a student at a game, I often show up at the last 30 minutes, sit with the parents, and then go high five the student at the end of the game. The parents think I'm awesome, and as far as the student is concerned, I might as well have been there the entire time. Score!

Monitor your default. As a guy with a youth ministry background, it's easy for me to gravitate to students. It takes some intentionality for me to invest in relationships with parents and volunteers. Over the years though, this tendency has become much easier to manage.

Recruit Parents to Communicate for You

A number of years ago we experienced a tragedy that turned into an incredible work of God. I met a student in our youth ministry who had a passion for missions and serving and would do anything to make others laugh. His humor and mischievousness was well-known to all. Tragically on a sunny Sunday evening in September, his life was cut short in a car accident while he was on his way to his girlfriend's youth group.

That week, in a packed auditorium full of families and countless high school students, his dad gave a wonderful message that stirred people to tears and laughter, sometimes both at the same time. What was so powerful that day was the way in which his dad depicted his love for missions and serving. I would never have predicted what would happen in the months to come as we planned a mission trip for the following summer. Not only had the youth ministry grown significantly in the midst of tragedy, but we also found ourselves planning a mission trip for a gigantic number of students as well as his mom, dad, and two sisters. God had indeed begun to show us how he can use a human tragedy to make an eternal difference.

As I sat down with my team, I wondered how we could possibly create a manageable way to raise funds for such a large number of people. Then there was the question of communication. How on earth could we communicate with so many families? It was a task of massive proportions that I'd never encountered before. We needed help. Specifically we needed parents to help communicate the details and to get other parents and their kids to attend the mission trip meetings.

What happened is we pinpointed five or six parents who were well-established and known in our church. I asked them if they would be the ones to make phone calls, answer questions, and help plan the mission team meetings. To my surprise, they all said yes. They were so excited to support such an incredible move of God. All I needed to do was provide the contact information for all the families and the information for the trip. From there, they made the calls, answered questions, and reminded parents about the times and dates for the meetings. And wouldn't you know it, we had nearly 100 percent attendance at the missions meetings and a surplus of funds.

The fruit of recruiting parents to communicate with other parents is that they'll take ownership of the ministry with greater zeal and excitement. When that happens, they also become your best promoters.

Make Use of Social Media

I've been blogging for the better part of six years now, and I think I've adapted well to utilizing social media for my blog. I've also reaped the benefits of utilizing social media to communicate the vision and details of my ministries. I know this isn't the case for all of my fellow church workers. I have friends who tell me they don't have time to be following their friends' latest posts detailing what they had for breakfast. I understand where they're coming from to a degree. At the same time, though, they're missing out on a valuable way to communicate with parents and their kids both the vision and details about their ministry.

The fact is, social media is here to stay, and it's a mode of communication that the upcoming generations are flocking to. It's also a mode parents are flocking to if they're monitoring their kids' activity on the Internet. And quite frankly, many parents are just as addicted to social media as their kids are.

So how can we make the most of social media in our ministries? Here are a few thoughts.

Only post what's helpful. One of the keys to keeping parents engaged is to ensure that your communication is helpful to them and is something they'll want to keep coming back to. Provide information that helps and supports parents, such as articles on parenting or using social media or

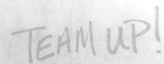

insightful statistics on raising children. Also comment in your posts about what you think is most helpful about the resources you share. A few words from you will make the communication stick with greater effectiveness, and your words will become another way to pursue your vision of reaching and equipping the next generation by equipping parents.

Create dialogue. I spend quite a lot of time on social media. There's a plethora of quirky and funny pictures, great quotes to be inspired by, and even some articles by people in ministry. But for me one of the best things about social media is that I get to engage with some great people who are in the trenches of ministry, just like I am. The problem is, there are many who just want to post their latest article in the hopes that I'll read it. They're not really interested in talking about what they've posted. While I'm always interested in reading articles and hearing new ideas, it's so much easier to engage with content from people who've taken the time to create a two-way dialogue. This is true for parents as well. While it's great to post information, articles, and resources, it's essential to ask questions and create conversations with the people you expect to read your posts.

In my experience, creating conversation on social media works best by asking simple questions that appeal to a wide range of people. Here are some examples of things I've asked parents in the past:

- What is your family doing for the holidays?
- What family traditions do you have for Christmas?
- What are some favorite summer outings you've taken with your family?
- What's one thing you're doing to help your kids talk about God at home?
- What's one thing your kids love about kids' church or youth group?
- What advice would you give to parents who are barely keeping up with their crazy schedules?

Respond to comments and questions. Conversation is a two-way street. As you consider how to engage with parents on social media, ensure that you're responding to their comments and questions and not just expecting them to respond to yours. An unanswered comment or post can be like ignoring a parent in the hallway at church. While it takes some time out of our schedules, posting a response is a valuable way of building rapport with the parents who entrust their kids to us each week.

Guard your time. Social media can take over your life if you're not careful. Maybe you've already learned that the hard way. For some it's not hard to while away hours checking in on social media feeds and then suddenly realize they haven't gotten anything done. For those who would describe themselves as social media-inept, the wasted hours can go to just trying to figure out what they're doing. And then there are those for whom the idea of using social media seems like a great waste of time overall.

In a world where more and more parents and their kids are using social media as their primary platform for communication, it's crucial that we begin to communicate in the spaces they occupy. The great news is that with a few simple steps, you can make social media work for you without getting either consumed or overwhelmed by it.

Consolidate your postings. I currently use a social media management tool that allows me to create posts that go out over numerous social networks at the same time. If you're going to use social media effectively—whether you're social media-savvy or not—using this kind of tool is vital. It'll save you valuable time. I could give you the names of some of the tools I use, but chances are there's an even better one that's been developed since I wrote this. The best way to find a good tool is to type "social media management tool" into the search field of your web browser. You'll find a long list of articles that give reviews on the latest and best ones to use.

Schedule in advance. If you're busy like I am, it's often challenging to keep up with consistently posting information for parents to view. It's also a fact that the content you and I post will be in parents' feeds for a short amount of time, and then it won't show up again. A good social media management tool can help you deal with those things, too. It'll enable you to easily schedule the delivery of content throughout the week and only have to think about it once. My youth pastor would say that he's not the most social media-savvy guy around. Even though he's quite a bit younger than me, he never seemed to get into the world of social media. However, he understands that his students and parents are spending a lot of time engaging with social media, and it's become an essential platform for him to utilize. That's why every Monday he schedules his posts, texts, and emails to go out during the week. Apart from checking in to reply to questions or comments, he doesn't have to think about posting for the rest of the week.

Post pictures. It's great to communicate about programs and events, but there's nothing better than posting photos of kids having a blast in your

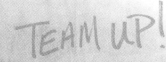

ministry. If you want to keep parents coming back to your page, give them more than just information. Give them the smiles, laughter, and excitement found in the photos of their kids. Pictures can create engagement and excitement for your ministry. But beware! Before posting pictures of kids, ensure that you have permission from parents. We include a place on all our registration and medical waiver forms for parents to grant their permission for us to post pictures of their kids.

I used to take it personally when parents didn't read my emails or know about an event I had painstakingly planned for them or their kids. I've met countless children's and youth ministry workers who've wondered if parents really care. Even worse, there have been times I've wondered if parents were simply choosing to ignore me. What I've found is that it all comes down to whether or not I'm communicating effectively. Whether I'm intentionally getting my message out with enough frequency and variety to break through the promotion dilution experienced by parents today. Whether I'm taking the time to get to know parents and their needs and preferences the way I need to. If I'm getting those things right, I can be confident parents will receive the information they need for me to partner with them effectively.

GAME PLAN SUMMARY

In a world of competing messages, it's imperative to communicate strategically, simply, and consistently.

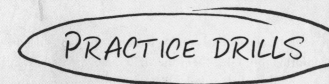

PRACTICE DRILLS

*Use the following action steps to help you apply
what you've learned to your life and ministry.*

1. Take 10 minutes to create a basic communication plan for your ministry. What are
   some things you can do to communicate on a weekly basis? monthly? yearly? Look
   back through the chapter if you need ideas. In the next week, run your plan by two or
   three other team members, volunteers, or parents for their feedback. Then choose one
   item from your plan, and begin to implement it.

2. Take a look at the social media networks you currently use. Search the Internet for
   articles and resources that could help you improve the way in which you use social
   media for your ministry. How could you use social media for communicating information about your ministry or upcoming events? What resources could you best provide
   the parents in your ministry via social media?

3. Create a small card to hand out to parents that they can complete in a minute or less.
   Include a place for them to write their name, email address, phone numbers, the social
   media they use, and their preferred modes of communication.

4. Evaluate how much of your time is given to investing relationally in parents. What
   can you do to improve the way you go about building relationships with parents?
   What's one thing you can do this week to build rapport with one of the parents in your
   ministry?

5. Create a list of responsibilities you typically have on a Sunday morning. Identify one or
   two of those responsibilities you could hand off to someone in order to make time for
   connecting with parents and the people you could hand those things off to. Contact
   those people, and begin planning for them to take over those responsibilities.

TEAM UP!

Chapter 6

PROVIDE RESOURCES

*Be an expert at helping parents
find answers rather than one who's
expected to have the answers.*

"**H**ow can I talk to my kids about sex?" That was the question
(or something like it) one of my best volunteers asked me
a number of years ago. To be honest, I still can't recall his exact words simply
because I was so stunned that he'd even asked. At the time, I looked up to
him as a wise and God-honoring man who seemed to have life figured out.
I didn't have any kids then, and the idea of having kids myself was a little
intimidating. It wouldn't be long before I'd be asking him how to survive the
early, sleepless years of being a new parent. So why would he ask me such
a heavy question that I felt so unqualified to answer? As I reflected on this
and many similar questions over the years, I've learned an extremely valuable
lesson that's improved the way I minister to parents ever since. No matter
how inadequate I may feel, parents see me as the go-to expert in matters
involving their kids. The same is true for you.

You're the expert whether you know it or not. It doesn't matter if
you're a volunteer or paid staff. It doesn't matter if you're single or married
or whether you have kids or not. The fact that you've chosen to be active
in the field of children's, youth, or family ministry automatically qualifies
you in the eyes of parents. I know there'll be some parents who'll always

see you as the baby sitter to their kids, but there's a greater number of parents who'll look to you for answers and expertise. You might not be an expert in parenting, but you're well on your way to becoming an expert on kids—or at least that's how parents will view you if you stick around for a while.

It's nice to have others see us as the experts. But what happens when the rubber meets the road? What happens when parents really need an answer from you, and you simply have no idea? The good news is that being an expert doesn't mean that parents really expect you to have all the answers, but they're hoping you can help them find good answers. On top of that, most parents understand that you're busy and there may be too much content to cover in the time you have available. There have been many times a parent has made the assumption that I'm busy with their kids and have little time for them. Not long ago a parent said to me, "I know you're busy. Can you point me to something that will help me understand technology better? My kids are online more and more, and I want to keep them safe." By pointing parents to resources, you're actually able to give them relatively short answers while still giving them the information they need.

Become a Student of Resources

As someone who works with children and students, you'll naturally have greater access to resources than many of your parents will ever be aware of. It's imperative that you and I become eyes and ears for parents regarding what's available to them. Let's look at some different ways you can build a list of resources to suggest to parents.

Ask your peers. The other children's and youth ministry workers you know have experience you can draw from, both in ministry and as parents themselves. Chances are they know of books, websites, and articles that are helpful for parents. When I was creating content for a parent workshop, I sent about 10 messages to friends of mine who are also in ministry and asked them to tell me what they considered to be the best resources for the topic the workshop was on. Within a day or so, I had some solid resources that I was able to start reviewing and using. The great news is that a number of them referred me to the same resources, essentially giving me a solid endorsement. Being able to stand in front of parents and tell them that a

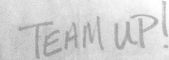

number of credible sources recommended a particular resource goes a long way when we don't have time to check out every resource ourselves.

Consult parents. There are parents in your ministry who are utilizing some great resources that you don't know anything about. In a previous church I met one mom who just loved to read and was fully invested in her child's faith journey. Over time I was able to recommend a number of resources that she had read and gained some great insights from. In fact, with her permission I was able to refer parents to her for certain questions that she had investigated for herself. In a way she became the parenting expert that other parents looked to for advice and resources. If you don't know who the parents like this are in your ministry, start asking parents what books or websites have been most helpful to them in their parenting, and why. If you have a social media page, you could post the question there. If not, find ways to weave it into conversations with parents you're getting to know.

Seek out professionals. Identify the professionals in your church or community who are trusted to help families. Include those who are highly regarded by others, such as Christian counselors, marriage and family therapists, and pediatricians. These are the people who'll have the best answers for the families you minister to. Your role is simply to refer parents to them. If you don't know who those people are, talk to the people in your church who've been around a while and can help you pinpoint good experts in the field of marriage and family. We have someone who oversees the care ministry in our church, and she's been here for well over 20 years. Not only does she know people in the community, but she automatically has a good understanding of which professionals would be the best fit for a given family. It's so helpful having someone who knows the reputation and regard of counselors and doctors in the area.

Create a resource file. Over time I've found it helpful to build up a file of resources and contacts for parents. There's no way in the world that I can remember all the books, websites, or people that would be helpful to recommend. Having a resource file gives me a place to keep all that information at my fingertips. One of my goals for the next year is to actually have a parent oversee my resource file and become the one who seeks out great resources to refer to parents. I currently have a mom who's passionate about partnering with parents and wants to help out in this way. Whether you have

HOW TO WRITE A RESOURCE REVIEW

As you consider asking parents to review resources, here are some guidelines to help them know what to look for.

- Who is the resource best suited for?
- Why is this resource helpful for parents to read/use?
- What about this resource was most helpful to you as a parent?
- Where can parents buy this resource? How much does it cost?
- Ask for the review to be under 400 words.

such a parent in your ministry or not, keeping a file of resources is still crucial.

Have parents review resources. Parents listen to parents. One of the most effective ways to provide helpful resources is to get a parent to read a book or to use a resource and then review it. Whether it's posted on social media, the church website, or in printed form, parents are more likely to utilize a resource that's endorsed by another parent. This is something I've done sporadically before but hope to add more regularly to my ministry in the next year.

Become a Giver of Resources

So often the time that's afforded us on a Sunday morning or during a midweek program is limited in terms of what we can say to parents. When parents come to me with a question, there's a tendency in me to want to answer their question and bring complete closure to the issue they're facing. But to provide adequate help to parents in a few minutes is unrealistic. Referring parents to a good resource is a better way to go, especially if you really don't have good knowledge on a particular subject or issue.

In addition to the resources you might be able to mention to parents off the cuff in a conversation, there are other ways you can make various resources readily available to parents.

Create a resource stand. At the entrances to our birth to kindergarten and our elementary environments we have a resource stand right at the check-in area. The stand has a number of books, some DVDs, calendar information, and parent take-home sheets for that week's kids' message. Having the stand right there in our check-in area allows parents to see helpful resources and calendar information every week when they drop their kids off. For a digital alternative, create a virtual resource stand on your church's website, and place signs in the check-in area of your building to let parents know how to access the information.

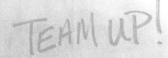

Provide a weekly take-home/parent page. A lot of curriculums are now providing a take-home sheet for parents that allows them to engage in the content throughout the week with their kids. If you don't have a resource like this, consider making it a part of your lesson creation each week. Providing parents with a bottom line from the lesson, the Bible verses used, and some questions they can ask their kids is a great start. But keep in mind the possibility that a take-home sheet might get left at church or in the family's minivan. Consider other ways to get it into parents' hands, or find creative ways to bring it to the focus of parents. You could send it as part of a weekly email or post it on the church website. Once it's home we've found that making it into a monthly laminated dinner place mat is a great way to make discussion questions part of family mealtimes.

Have kids give their parents "homework." This is one of the best ideas I've heard recently. What kid wouldn't want to give his or her parents an assignment to complete? Whether it's interacting with the take-home/parent page or reading an article, recruiting kids to assign something for their parents to do is a great way to resource parents.

Because I've been around a long time, there are many occasions a parent will ask a question to which I know the answer. However, it's crucial that I see my role as someone who equips parents rather than as someone who's quick to provide solutions. If I'm able to point them to a good book or article that gets them to dig deeper into an issue or question, it's far better than a quick answer in the hallway at church. It increases the likelihood that they'll own the information and answers they find. And you never know—they might even become good candidates for providing reviews and recommendations of resources for others.

GAME PLAN SUMMARY

By resourcing parents, you move from having to know all the answers to helping parents find the answers for themselves.

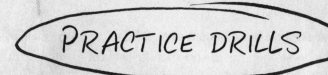

PRACTICE DRILLS

*Use the following action steps to help you apply
what you've learned to your life and ministry.*

1. Ask parents to identify their go-to websites for parenting help. Post the question on social media to increase your range of answers. Use the responses to create a list you can share with other parents. (You may want to do a brief check of the websites you include on the list—or have a trusted parent check them out—to make sure they're appropriate.)

2. Ask parents in your ministry to tell you what their felt needs are when it comes to the kind of resources they're looking for. Use their responses to guide you in your search for resources. Make a goal of finding at least two or three resources for each of the felt needs the parents identified.

3. If you have children, create a list of books, podcasts, or curriculums that you have benefited from and that you could share with parents. Make that list available on a resource stand, the church website, or via social media.

4. With their permission, publish a list of "experts" in your church who can be a resource for parents, including counselors, physicians, educators, and "been there" parents. Include a notice to parents clarifying that services are not free (unless otherwise noted) just because these individuals are part of the church and that appropriate compensation may be expected at the time of service.

5. Assemble a parent resource team to help you brainstorm different ways to provide resources for parents and creative ways to help parents continue spiritual conversations with their children at home.

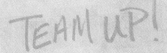

Chapter 7

EQUIP DISENGAGED PARENTS

*How to train and equip parents
when they won't even show up.*

There are times I feel as if being in ministry set me up with unrealistic expectations for raising kids of my own. Teaching someone else's kids is a piece of cake compared to teaching my own kids the simplest of things. When it's someone else's kids, it's easier to switch off, head home, and move on emotionally. Even when I've had a bad day in ministry and have had to deal with "that kid," I can still sleep relatively easily at night.

Having my own kids is a totally different ballgame. Being a dad has given me more gray hairs and has resulted in less hair overall. Some people call gray hair "a crown of wisdom." I call it a significant battle scar. My kids say I'm just getting old. I say they're the reason my crown is getting so thin. But I wouldn't change it for the world.

Being a parent is the most frustrating, rewarding, challenging, interesting, and joyous role I've ever entered into. I'm so thankful for the many people who have come alongside me as I've often bumbled my way through being a husband and father. In particular, I'm forever thankful to my friend and mentor Ron. Ron has been in ministry for 40 years or more (and is still going strong, he would add). I'm thankful for the wisdom and resources he's passed along to help me on my journey in marriage, parenting, and ministry. I know a lot about the latest resources that can help me in my own pursuit of being a good parent. But there's nothing quite like Ron coming alongside me to give me insights, tools, and the face-to-face encouragement that I really can do it.

All parents need someone to help and encourage them as they navigate through the journey of raising their kids. It's one thing to have resources. It's quite another thing to be equipped by people who are invested in you and your family. But if you don't have someone in your life to help equip you for marriage and family, you're in good company. That's the reality for many, if not most, parents.

Overcoming the Obstacles

Equipping and resourcing are vastly different things when it comes to partnering with parents. To state it simply, *resourcing* parents focuses on pointing parents to materials or helps they can utilize for themselves. *Equipping* parents involves developing their knowledge and skills by teaching, training, and encouraging them. Every parent in your ministry needs greater equipping and support, and you might be the best person to help in that area.

When I was in my early years of ministry, the idea of equipping parents wouldn't have been on my radar. If someone came along and wrote a book like this and attempted to convince me to provide parent training or seminars, I'd have skipped to the next chapter citing that I was too young and inexperienced to do such a thing.

If you're a children's ministry veteran reading this, you might have already attempted some kind of seminar and given up following a low turnout that consisted of the parents who already "get it." A friend who was also in children's ministry had this to say to me a number of years ago:

> "Parent meetings and parent seminars are a waste of time! No one shows up to them and even if you can get parents to show up, they're usually the ones who are already making an attempt to do the right things. What about all the parents who don't know or don't care? How can I help them?"

 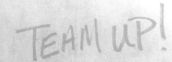

Quite frankly, I had to agree with him. In my experience it had always been challenging to get parents to show up to an informational meeting, and it was even more challenging to get them to show up for a parent seminar. Since my conversation with my friend, parents—in my opinion—have only become more stressed and overscheduled. Why would they ever be interested in a training seminar?

While I'd all but given up trying to get parents to show up for meetings and seminars, my push-back to my friend was:

> "But there's got to be a way to engage parents and give them the tools they need to raise their kids. It's too important to simply give up. They're with their kids so much more than we are. They have greater influence and impact on their kids! We've got to find a way in!"

I'd previously had many other conversations that were pushing me toward approaching the issue differently. But this was the conversation that made me say, "That's it! I've got to do this!"

I later had my opportunity. I was a new guy in a completely new role. My new church had never had a family ministry pastor before. As a church they had some incredible ministry environments from birth through high school, and they had a wonderfully innovative family ministry team, which I was now charged to lead. The children's and youth ministries were, as a whole, working as a cohesive team. My role would be to lead the team to greater cohesion, help rebuild a struggling youth ministry, and—here's the exciting part—develop and implement a strategic plan to partner with parents.

I essentially had a blank canvas and a great deal of freedom and trust. If there was ever a time to try something new or tweak something old, it had come. This British Bulldog was determined to reach and equip parents to raise their kids with a solid faith foundation through an experiment called ParentWise. Motivated by my prior experience with poorly attended parent meetings and my friend's comments about such meetings being a waste of time, I began pursuing the goal of creating a series of seminars for three groups of parents: parents of children birth through kindergarten, parents of elementary-aged children, and parents of middle school and high school students.

When I first started to dream up ParentWise, I kept referring to it as an "experiment" as a way to cover my bases just in case it failed. (If you ever hear a leader refer to a new ministry or program as an experiment, you can be quite sure that leader has no idea how it's really going to turn out.) To call ParentWise an experiment might suggest that I jumped in without having a plan or purpose, but that was far from the truth. Since the conversation with my friend about the value of parent meetings, I'd given a great deal of thought to how best to reach and equip parents. I was especially driven by one crucial question: How could I reach those parents who hadn't traditionally shown up for meetings and seminars?

Lessons to Learn From

I always thought there was a magic bullet to reaching parents; that I'd go to a conference and discover some innovative idea that would solve all my problems. Sometimes when things aren't working in ministry, there's this tendency to gravitate to the latest thing or implement something that worked in a church somewhere else without considering how it will work in our own contexts. Consequently, there's also a tendency to overlook simple answers that were there all along. But the truth is, much of what I've discovered—and am still discovering—really isn't rocket science. Simply put, what my team has achieved through ParentWise is largely built around common sense and a willingness to evaluate and adapt.

I used to think that parent seminars were outdated and the goal of reaching and equipping parents was unreachable. Our experience with ParentWise changed that perspective. Attendance was much better than I had ever experienced, and the feedback we got from parents was not only positive, but it included requests to cover other areas of parenting as well. We also saw parents join small groups with other parents they had connected with at ParentWise. That wasn't something we had planned; it just happened. And it makes me wonder what would've been the outcome if we had better planned that next step for parents.

With those things in mind, what follows are some of the key lessons I learned about equipping parents from developing and implementing ParentWise. If you grab on to them, they'll offer you the ability to reach and equip parents in ways that can be implemented wherever you are.

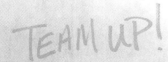

Listen to parents. Equipping isn't primarily about you or me; it's about parents. I'm sure we both know that, but so often what we attempt to provide parents is more about us and our agenda for them than it is about their genuine needs and concerns. From the perfectly planned presentation for getting parents to buy into our ministries to the parent workshop focused on making church a greater priority, we can tend to be motivated by what's in it for us.

Now there's nothing inherently wrong with those kinds of meetings. Sometimes they're necessary. But they're not going to draw a crowd. And let's be honest, the parents who do show up at those meetings usually show up for everything you do anyway. With that in mind, what does it take to get parents intrigued enough to give time to show up at a meeting or seminar? What I've discovered is that they'll give their time when we take time to invest in their felt needs.

Just take a moment to think about the parents in your ministry. What are their greatest needs? What are their greatest struggles as parents? What do they wish someone would tell them?

Now maybe I'm just a little slow on the uptake, but for so many years I had looked for ideas to engage parents with information and support in ways I thought would be helpful. However, it never occurred to me to ask them what would be most helpful. Maybe as a younger leader I was afraid to ask, or maybe I thought I knew what they needed. Either way, in my busyness I never slowed down enough to consider what parents really needed from me. Perhaps deep down inside I didn't consider that I could actually help parents (especially in my early years when I was single and didn't have kids). However, as I took time to sit down and talk with parents, I discovered an essential key to partnering with them: listening. So much of ministry emphasizes how you and I speak and communicate. Yet listening well to parents is the first step on the path to partnering with them. That's because listening builds bridges of trust.

Until I had my own kids, I never understood the feelings of insecurity most parents feel from day to day. Most parents I meet are all too aware of their own flaws and those of their kids. Many of them live in the unrealistic hope that you and I will never discover the real family that lives behind the forced church smile. I know this feeling all too well.

It's a Sunday morning, and we're running late. Our youngest still has food all over his face, our oldest has changed her outfit at least three times, and our middle child is determined to do the opposite of whatever Lisa or I ask. The instructions to hurry up are no longer polite requests—they've turned into bloodcurdling tirades that are likely being heard by parts of our neighborhood. We jump into a minivan that's a perfect representation of our lives—it looks like someone stocked it full of diapers, toys, candy wrappers, and old socks and then threw in a hand grenade. As we drive a mile to church, the chaos continues as the kids bicker and whine, and Lisa and I dissect who's to blame for being late—yet again. We arrive at church, the van doors open, and immediately we all jump into church mode and the forced Sunday smiles appear again. What would happen if people really found out about my imperfect family?

I've come to realize that I can't really hide my family flaws, and it doesn't help others be honest about their struggles when I try. There are parents throughout our churches who are attempting to hide their family flaws and keep up appearances while feeling absolutely isolated and alone. That's why it's imperative that you and I live with openness about our own challenges. It helps them realize we're flawed, too. We also need to take time to listen to parents' real concerns and discover the real people behind the facades. When we open up our lives to parents and take time to listen to them, we're helping them be real as well, and we're ultimately building bridges of trust between us and them.

Someone once said, "Speak in such a way that others love to listen to you. Listen in such a way that others love to speak to you." By leaning in and listening to what's important to parents, we also begin to gain vital insights into their most pressing concerns. And those insights are what enable us to create meetings and seminars parents will want to give their time to because they know they'll receive content they need to hear.

Address parents' present concerns. Most parents are living in survival mode and want answers for the most pressing issues of the day. We need to create seminars and meetings for parents centered on those issues. Recently I did a parent workshop called "Parenting in Survival Mode" for parents of elementary-age kids. For families with kids at that age, schedules are starting to pick up the pace, and there seems to be a never-ending list of activities (and expenses) for parents. Parents in this

 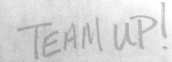

season of life feel as if they're barely treading water most of the time, and survival has very possibly taken the place of passing on faith to their kids. They're looking for someone to help them slow down, take a deep breath, and focus. With a captive audience, this was a great opportunity to cast a Deuteronomy 6:4-9 vision and give some simple and practical steps for utilizing teachable times and creating intentional moments without adding to an already maxed-out schedule.

Create a parent team. It's always easier to do things myself. It can get messy when others are involved. And involving parents in particular can take things to a whole new level of messiness. So why would I want to recruit parents to help me? One word: ownership. When parents are involved they take on a vested interest in seeing the activities they're a part of succeed. When that happens, parents also become natural promoters of those activities, increasing the potential reach of those things. That's true whether the activities are events and programs for kids or parent seminars. Greater ownership produces greater results. When what we're doing is simply "our thing," parents won't make as much of an investment. But when it's "their thing," they'll be inclined to make a greater effort and help others do the same.

The other benefit that comes with involving parents in what you do is the ability to delegate. While that requires some added communication on your part, it also frees you up to focus on assembling and delivering the content at a meeting without being consumed with the nuts and bolts of planning and implementation as well. As you recruit parents to help you put on meetings and seminars, be thinking about people who can help you promote the event, greet participants and help them get registered, serve refreshments, provide child care, and even present content. By getting people plugged in to just those simple, strategic roles, you've lightened your load and increased the number of people committed to seeing the meeting succeed.

Utilize parents and other experts. One of the struggles I've faced in considering how to equip parents is feeling like I have to know it all. I'll never have enough time or experience to equip parents in every area in which they need help. That's a reality for all of us in ministry. The great news is that you and I don't have to know it all. In fact, I've discovered it's actually to my advantage to have experts and peers create and deliver content rather than trying to do it all myself. I'm not talking about paying a speaker thousands of dollars to come in and speak to parents. I'm talking about involving people who are in your community and in your church. Let me give you a couple of examples.

Recently we provided two workshops to parents of middle school and high school students. We surveyed parents, and the clear message we got was that they needed help protecting their kids in regard to technology and drugs. Not too long before, some students in the community had been in trouble for "sexting," and a recent graduate had died from a heroin overdose. Many parents were overwhelmed with fear and concern for their kids as a result. I knew I had to do something to address those concerns. But here was the problem: I didn't have time to create content, and I certainly didn't have the expertise to provide anything of significance to my parents. As I talked with some key parents and staff at my church, we were able to pinpoint some people and organizations nearby that had expertise in these areas of need.

After a number of phone calls and "getting to know you" meetings (don't miss this step), I was able to recruit a local school drug counselor, a drug task force detective, and a police detective who was an expert in technology. All I really had to do was give them a good picture of what I was looking for, a sense of what to expect from our parents, and some guidelines for time and how the workshop would run. And here's the best part: there was no cost to bring them in. What I discovered as I made phone calls to the local schools, police departments, and counselors is that it's in their interests to get out into the community. It was also essential to talk to my church leadership and ensure they were in support of the speakers I was looking to bring in. For me, that was no problem. In fact, when the drug task force detective asked permission to bring "samples" of drugs into the workshop, my executive director fully supported the idea. Now just in case you are wondering what I mean by "samples," let me be clear. The samples were purely for parents to look at in order for them to understand what drugs look like and how they're packaged.

Perhaps the most startling thing about utilizing experts is how they can become a great promotional draw. While I like to think that parents love the quirky English guy, they'd rather hear from an expert on a drug task force or an expert in technology. What's more, given that we weren't providing any Christian content in the workshops, the local

TEAM UP!

school system actually provided promotion for us through its newsletters and regular emails. Both workshops were very well attended, and we had a large number of people from our community who had never been to our church—or any church at all. How about that? The drug counselor shared that this was the largest group of parents he'd ever spoken to and loved how invested our church was. It was also a great bridge builder with the school system. It opened up the opportunity for me to be part of an advisory committee and panel of presenters for a parent workshop they were holding on bullying. How about that? I had a plan, but God had a bigger plan.

An example of someone in my church who was able to present content to parents is Mike. I met Mike quite early on at my present church. He's a parent and a great guy with an incredibly positive attitude that's just infectious. He's also a great husband and father. Everything I've observed about him and the way he lives out his faith is absolutely authentic. What's more is that others hold him in high regard and look to him as a leader in our church. That's one of the reasons I sought him out to grab a coffee a couple of years ago. As we talked faith, family, and his work, we got back to the subject that most people ask me about: "How is ministry going for you?" That particular week I was in the beginning stages of creating content for a workshop called "Parenting for Purity." As we talked, Mike shared some steps he had taken with each of his sons that had become defining milestones in their faith journeys and had also helped them understand God's plan for sexuality. It suddenly hit me that other parents needed to hear Mike's story. So a month later I interviewed Mike as he shared some practical and specific steps he used to talk to his kids about sex.

There's a twofold lesson I learned from having Mike share. First, since Mike is in the trenches of parenting teenagers, his story held more weight than anything I could have shared. Second, there are a lot more "Mikes" in our church who've navigated through certain seasons of raising kids and have come out the other side with wisdom and hope to offer. One such parent in our church is Trish. She came to me a number of months ago and expressed her heart to partner with parents and pass on what she'd learned on her parenting journey so far. (When people keep hearing the vision from you and me, they'll come and seek us out when it captures their heart.) Now Trish is helping me equip and train parents with kids from birth through elementary age.

You and I can't be experts in everything, but there are people in your community and church who can lend their expertise and experience to providing great content that'll help equip parents. They'll also likely draw greater numbers than you or I can.

Schedule strategically. One of the biggest reasons parent workshops fail is poor scheduling. It's not because they aren't valuable or important. A few years ago I attended a friend's church that had flown in a nationally acclaimed speaker for a parenting seminar. While it was a great parenting seminar, I was somewhat shocked that more parents didn't show up for those few hours on a Saturday morning. In trying to think of what kept people from being there, kids' Saturday morning sports, weekend projects, and family time were just a few of the conflicts I could come up with. And while those things didn't seem like significant conflicts to me, they were significant in the community in which my friend ministered.

One of the reasons parents don't attend parenting workshops is simply because they don't have margin to add another thing into their schedules. In between work, their kids' schedules, and their typical family rhythms, it's hard to expect them to show up on another evening of the week— or perhaps their only free evening of the week—to be a family together. Therefore, it's imperative to schedule times of equipping when they're naturally and normally on campus at our churches. Parents of young kids find it difficult to show up to a midweek parent workshop because meal-times and bedtimes are a limiting factor. Parents of middle school and high school students barely have another night of the week available as they're living in taxi-driver mode during the week. So the question we have to ask ourselves is, "Given our church schedules, when are these two parent groups naturally and normally at church?" And the answer to that question has to drive the way in which we schedule events for parents.

At my church, parents of younger children are around on Sunday mornings, so that's often the best time to provide a parent workshop. While it's limited and short, it's far better than a longer time frame for which no one shows up. Our middle school and high school students meet on a Wednesday night for their large-group programs. While many parents use this time to go grocery shopping or get laundry done while their kids are busy, for many others it's an open evening since they have to come to the church to drop off and pick up their kids anyway. Last year we

 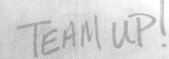

provided four workshops on Wednesday evenings that were well attended and well received since they didn't require parents to drastically change their schedules.

Provide community, not just content. One of the greatest ways you and I can support parents is to help them get connected with each other. Many parents feel as though they have to keep up appearances. Consequently, they also feel alone and think that other parents are getting it right while they're getting it all wrong. It's not until they get to sit around a table and talk to other parents that they realize they're not alone and that there are many other parents who feel just as messed up as they do. That's why it's essential to create opportunities in workshops for parents to talk with each other about the content. Not only does it help them apply what they're hearing, it enables them to connect with and build community with other parents as well. In the last year I've seen friendships and supportive relationships begin at a workshop and continue after it's over and done.

Give options. No matter what you do, there will never be a good way to reach everyone and get every parent to a workshop. That's why we need to provide other ways for parents to receive training and information. For our middle school and high school workshops, we received a number of requests to record the content so parents could watch it later. If you aren't tech savvy, that could be a challenge. But there may be people in your church who know how to do that stuff and would be happy to help. Even better, there might be a parent who could become a part of your team to help you record and post the content.

As my team looks ahead, this is one area that we're exploring more and more. Eventually we hope to create a series of videos that'll be available for parents to view at their convenience. We might lose some ability to build community that way, but it's better than a parent missing the content entirely.

It's possible that you aren't at a point of being able to create workshops yet. Don't worry—that used to be me, too. However, consider some of the small steps you can take to equip parents in being the primary investors in their child's faith journey:

- Refer parents to books and videos that could be helpful to them.
- Encourage parents to get involved in small groups or classes that are designed to equip parents.

- Seek out empty nesters or veteran parents who could serve as mentors to parents who are looking for help.
- Promote parent workshops at other churches in your area.

Every parent needs help somewhere along the way. We can provide that help by equipping parents for the journey. When we schedule strategically, provide content that meets parents' felt needs, and involve others in the process, we can create opportunities for equipping parents that they'll want to be a part of.

GAME PLAN SUMMARY

The biggest hurdle to equipping parents is getting them to show up, and to clear that hurdle we have to put their needs—not ours—first.

TEAM UP!

PRACTICE DRILLS

Use the following action steps to help you apply what you've learned to your life and ministry.

1. Create a survey to learn about the felt needs of the parents in your church. Ask questions about the kinds of topics they would like to learn about or struggles they could use help with the most. Based on the survey results, create a training seminar or workshop to address the most frequently mentioned felt needs.

2. Take a look at your typical church schedule, and brainstorm with some of the parents in your ministry times that would be good for providing a parent seminar or workshop. Consider when parents are naturally and normally coming to your church. Then pencil a workshop into your calendar and begin planning for it.

3. Create a list of experts and parent peers in your community and church who could lead or teach in a workshop. Begin contacting those people to discuss the possibility of working with them to put on a parent-equipping event.

4. Create a list of roles parents could fill that would enable them to take ownership of a parent-equipping event. Then identify the key parents in your ministry who could fill those roles. Contact those parents, and ask them to prayerfully consider participating.

5. If creating a series of workshops isn't an option for you right now, identify one thing you could do to help equip the parents in your ministry—and begin doing it. Look back through the chapter for additional ideas.

6. Identify opportunities in your community or through other churches or organizations for parents to receive training, and promote them in your church's bulletin, website, or social media network.

Chapter 8

HAVE AN
INTENTIONAL
MINISTRY
STRATEGY

*How a clear strategy for
ministry helps you
partner with parents.*

I used to think that being a nice guy with a cool British accent was all I needed in ministry. That I would just have to open my mouth and word would get out about the guy with the great accent. That I could just throw out a few typically British phrases, people would trust me, and I could get parents to say yes to anything. After all, doesn't having an English accent make me trustworthy?

The answer to that is no. Relying on something like an accent is just shallow. In fact, when I get free stuff because of my accent, my wife reminds me of how shallow it really is.

Being a really nice person isn't a bad thing. And I'm told that having an accent makes me sound more intelligent. But parents (and their kids) need more than nice people and British accents to reach the next generation for Christ. They need a compelling vision and—more importantly—a strategy that can make that vision a reality.

In the last decade or so, vision statements were a big deal in the church. The most successful churches seemed to have well-crafted statements that would communicate what they saw as a hoped-for future. Church leaders would ask the people in the church to commit to and even memorize those statements. (That wasn't for me, by the way. Bible memorization is enough of a challenge for me. Don't make me memorize statements as well.)

In more recent years churches have also added catchy taglines that capture people's attention and quickly communicate a church's most important values. Such taglines often strive to let visitors know what to expect from the church as well.

As great as vision statements and taglines are, what gives them their power is having a strategy that enables you to live them out. Strategy is what tells you the steps you must take to move intentionally toward your hoped-for future or to put your most important values into practice. Vision statements and taglines only buy you time as you work toward seeing them become reality. People need to see constant movement toward the vision and to be reminded that each step moves them strategically closer to it.

There are plenty of things that happen by accident. But the greatest things happen when we take a God-given vision and prayerfully consider how to act on it. That's what this chapter is all about.

Effective Strategies Build Confidence and Trust

If a compelling vision serves to capture the hearts of families in our churches, then a healthy strategy is what builds trust and confidence as parents and kids see that vision at work. Parents won't continue to send their kids to you just because people tell them you're really nice. Parents want to know the why and how of your ministry, too. When they see a plan that's in place and a strategy that's working, they're more likely to take you seriously.

Strategy also opens the door for parents to take greater ownership of reaching and equipping their kids for Christ. Once parents get involved in your ministry and see its inner workings, having a healthy strategy they can get behind will encourage them to get even more involved and invest in the lives of their kids. Haphazardness can hinder parents' willingness

to partner with you. But having a clear strategy can open the doorway to parents letting you come alongside them to help them invest in their child's faith journey.

Depending on your ministry culture and your community, it's likely that certain strategies will be more effective than others. What works in my context might not work at all in your context. However, when it comes to partnering with parents in reaching and equipping the next generation for Christ, there are some strategies that I believe are universal.

Have a Synchronized Team Approach

Let's take a moment to revisit the rowing illustration from the beginning of Chapter 1. I mentioned how important it is for a rowing team to be synchronized and row in the same direction. It's so important, in fact, that there's a little guy at the back of the boat whose primary responsibilities are to steer the boat and keep the team in sync. He's called the coxswain or the cox. I used to think he was just a bossy boots who was there to tell the others to row faster. As a kid I used to imagine that he had a button that would give the rowers an electric shock if they weren't going fast enough. However, it turns out that what he's really doing is coordinating the power and rhythm of the rowers by giving them clear instructions and keeping them motivated. At the end of the race, the big, burly rowers on the winning team grab this little guy and throw him so that he goes high up into the air and then down into the murky brown River Thames. (That was always my favorite part.)

If rowing is an analogy for the local church, many of us find ourselves in a boat with a group of rowers who are out of sync with one another. As a result, we find ourselves going around in circles rather than moving forward. We paddle furiously in opposite directions, not even trying to coordinate our efforts. We see this most in the silo mentality that exists between our children's and youth ministries. They end up being either in competition with one another or so isolated from each other that there's no sense of continuity when children graduate from the children's ministry into the youth ministry. When it comes to reaching and equipping the next generation, there's no room for silos.

You probably have some good people on your team who have their oars in the water and are working hard toward a common vision. And you probably have some people who are paddling furiously in other, competing directions, making it hard for you to get anywhere. You also may have some people who've given up paddling altogether and feel as though they're aimlessly floating along, wondering where you all are heading. Unfortunately, that third perspective can carry over and affect the confidence of the parents and kids in your ministry as well. When the people we lead begin to wonder what's going on, they can start to wander off—sometimes going to another church that seems to have a better plan, sometimes heading in the direction of unhealthy choices or behaviors, and sometimes wandering away from the church altogether. That's why it's imperative that we commit to being part of a synchronized team that's rowing in the same direction.

Let's take a look at what that means in practical terms.

Begin with yourself. It just seems easier to work in a silo. When we knock the ball out of the park in our ministry areas, everyone's happy and we get the credit. When things go bad and no one has come out of their silo to help, we've got somewhere to place the blame (other than ourselves). But taking all the credit is just selfish, and placing the blame on others rather than owning it ourselves is a sign of weak leadership. The fact is, keeping synchronized with the rest of the team begins and ends with us. God has called us to be a part of the body of Christ—to work toward the common goal of reaching and equipping the next generation for Christ. We can't cut ourselves off from the rest of the body; it's essential that we invest ourselves in helping the body function in unity. If that means building bridges with other ministry areas or leaders, it's our responsibility to initiate those steps. We can't wait on them. There's too much at stake.

Get everyone in the same room. Synchronized teams don't just happen by accident. They begin with people like you and me taking the initiative to get in the same room as other key players. In my current ministry, we have a monthly family ministry meeting that consists of the children's and youth ministry staffs. The meeting is focused on training, sharing pertinent information, and discussing upcoming events. As for getting in the same room, we have little choice since we all share one office together. There are times that causes distractions to get the better of me, but for the

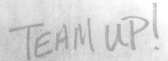

most part, it's a huge advantage having our team consistently working in the same physical space. You might not be part of a team like ours or even have an office, but that doesn't mean you can't find ways to get in the same room as your team members from time to time. It might mean hosting a team meeting in your home, getting together at a coffee shop, or meeting up at a park. With a little creativity, the options are endless.

Coordinate your calendars. There's nothing worse than one ministry area struggling because another ministry in your church scheduled a big event on the same date. Not only is it frustrating for leaders and volunteers who've poured their hearts and souls into an event or program, but it's also frustrating for a family who has to pick one event over another. In my church I have to ensure that I run every program and event through the keeper of the main church calendar first. Then I can coordinate with the children's and youth ministries. Sometimes that requires me to move an event for the betterment of the whole team. But that's what being a team player is all about. I tend to plan way in advance, but I realize that there are team members who aren't always inclined the same way. I can't just say, "I got the date first, so deal with it!" On the other hand, neither can I always be changing events at the last minute because someone else didn't plan well. That's where getting in the same room on a regular basis truly helps. It forces me to ask questions of my team members, consider their schedules, and evaluate how my schedule might help or hinder theirs.

Provide training and resources. Once a year we gather our family ministry volunteers all in the same room for training. While there's some training that's only relevant to volunteers working with certain age groups or ministry areas, there are other things that I want all of our family ministry volunteers to be exposed to regardless of the age they work with. That includes things like our vision, safety procedures, and how to partner with parents. Last year we also provided an emphasis on ministry for children and students with special needs. Since many of our volunteers have children and students with special needs integrated into their ministry environments, we wanted all of them to understand the basics of working with those kids. Utilizing the same training and resources in a large-group format for these kinds of topics is far more efficient and cost effective. It also ensures that the approach to those issues is common throughout all the age groups.

Our typical format for these yearly training meetings is to have a large-group session where, for about five to 10 minutes apiece, we cover the three or four key topics we want everyone to hear. Then we provide breakout sessions for volunteers in specific ministry areas from birth through high school. Here they're able to receive specific training for their areas, cover the calendar, pray for their kids, and build community with their teams. For example, last year the time devoted to breakout sessions was when the volunteers in One2One—our ministry specifically focused on special needs kids—received additional in-depth training for their area.

No matter what size church you come from, this kind of training is something that you could do in your context. And what's so brilliant about gathering all the volunteers together once a year is that it helps them see that they're all on the same team—whether they work with babies or high school students.

Creating a single training manual for all volunteers who work with ages birth through high school is another great way to ensure that all volunteers hear the same things and understand the same terms and language. Given that many volunteers in our church move up through the different age levels with the kids they lead, it's helpful to have the same practices and expectations across the board. It takes a little collaboration and makes for a larger manual than if we had one manual for the children's ministry and one for the youth ministry. However, having one manual for all ages can be a highly effective tool for keeping all your volunteers on the same page. There's no way I could cover every conceivable topic in a training manual. However, a combination of ideas and practices from different age levels will ensure that we're able to cover the essential bases for the children's and youth ministries while maintaining common language, terms, and best practices throughout.

Provide Consistency Between Age Levels

If the basic structure and format of your ministries is very different from one age group to another, it can become a stumbling block to helping kids stick around once they move up. Not only is it important for kids to experience things that are familiar from one age level to the next, it's essential to ensure that parents know how things work, too. In

TEAM UP!

my ministry we try to keep as many ministry components and people the same between age groups as possible so that it's not a completely different experience for children and students every time they move up. Here are a few ideas for ways you can do that in your ministry, too.

Encourage volunteers to move up. Haley has had Joanna* as her small-group leader since she was in third grade. Haley is now entering high school. With all the changes going on in high school, it's important that she's able to turn to a small-group leader who knows her and understands how to motivate her when challenges occur. Having Joanna as her small-group leader has often made all the difference for Haley, especially during some hard times in middle school.

While not every volunteer can move up with a group of children or students, it's certainly something we encourage whenever possible. Not only is there a great deal of trust built between a caring volunteer like Joanna and a child, but there's a natural relationship that begins to develop over the years between a volunteer and a parent. That's a huge win when we can accomplish it. Even a volunteer following kids through a few years will make an incredible difference and be a confidence booster for parents.

Include similar elements at each level. In my context I work with all ages up through high school. We have a similar structure to our environments at all age levels. It's not that we're trying to take a cookie-cutter approach or be controlling. We just know that kids and parents need some familiarity as their kids move up. For example, at the beginning of every experience there's a relational connecting time followed by a large-group message and a small-group experience. Apart from the very smallest ones, children in our ministry will always experience those three elements every time they gather. There are times in the year that we mix things up and create some alternative elements. But we know from experience that having similar elements and structures helps our kids stick around and feel comfortable.

Use common language and terms. As simple as it seems, there's great power in establishing a common language. Over time, using common terminology not only helps the team understand where the boat is heading, it also serves to build bridges between age-related environments as parents and kids transition from year to year. For example, if the preschool area is using different terminology than the elementary area is, or if the middle school area is using different terminology than the high school area is, it can muddy the vision and water down the strategy.

Know What Kids (and Their Parents) Want

Parents are influenced greatly by the opinions of their kids. Every year marketers spend massive amounts of money to capture the attention and commitment of kids, knowing it'll lead to gaining a greater share of the market for their products. And I'm not talking about them trying to get kids to buy the latest gadget, figure, or licensed product from the most recent Disney movie. I'm talking about stuff parents buy for themselves. Marketers use kids to influence their parents' purchasing decisions for everything from groceries to cars to apparel. The fact is, marketers know that kids have a great effect on their parents' purchasing decisions, both big and small. And this kind of influence isn't seen only in the world of marketers. If you look closely enough, you'll see how kids are influencing whether or not their parents will buy into your church.

I don't like using the term "buy into" when referring to the local church. For many years I've struggled with the way in which some churches have become commercialized, focusing more on numbers than on spiritual health and adopting more of a business mentality than a king-dom mentality. The church isn't supposed to be a business or a market-ing machine. But it's essential that we recognize we are in competition for the attention and commitment of kids and parents. Our willingness to engage in that competition can influence a family's decision to attend our church and affect our ability to reach kids with the gospel. When we create ministries that kids love to attend and a strategy that parents can easily commit to, we'll be better able to partner with parents in passing on the faith to the next generation.

What parents want for their kids. "Tell me, what brought you here?" That was the question I asked a single mom not long ago as she stood in the lobby of our church with three kids hanging on her legs. Her answer confirmed what I'd observed for some time: It was all about her kids. "I was talking with my friend who started coming here a few months ago. Her kids love coming, and they always have an incredible experience. Your

TEAM UP!

church isn't the kind of church I would normally attend, but I need to be somewhere my kids want to keep coming back to."

After speaking to this mom a little more, I discovered that her church background was quite different from the kind of experience we offer. She'd grown up with a traditional background and was more familiar with a liturgical worship service. We tend to be described in our community as "the church with loud music and lights." For someone coming from a background such as this mom had, I can only imagine that it was a bit of a shock to the system. But she was allowing herself to get an earache at our church simply because she thought it was what was best for her kids.

The fact is, parents today are determining where they live and what they do based on what's best for their kids and to give their kids positive feelings and experiences. It's not that parents didn't care before, but in recent years we've seen more parents going to greater lengths to ensure their kids are given the finest opportunities in every area of their lives. This isn't always a positive thing, and it can be taken to an extreme. But we have to understand that parents are looking to their kids for cues when it comes to where they'll commit. The stereotypical baby boomer parents were ultra-focused on their own accomplishments (often to the detriment of their kids). Today we're seeing the pendulum swing the other way as a greater number of younger parents are investing greater amounts of time and resources into their kids' lives. That's true when it comes to faith as well. Even though we meet many parents who don't necessarily know what to say or do in raising their kids with a solid faith, one thing is common: When it comes to the faith of their kids, parents are looking for a church that their kids love to attend.

Depending on the demographic of the families you work with, many of our parents are also stretched by increasing work pressures and are unable to invest in their kids as much as they'd like. Just recently I spoke to a single mom who shared that her only hour of solace during the week is at church. While she'd like to provide much more for her kids, she's barely treading water as it is, and she's desperate for support.

Parents like this mom find it hard to see the big picture of investing in their child's faith since they're living in survival mode most of the time. So often a perceived lack of drive on the part of parents regarding spiritual matters can easily be interpreted as not caring about their child's spiritual journey. But for many parents, just trying to find a safe place to drop their kids off to learn about God is about as far as they can see. Their efforts to get their kids to church at all can be a great starting point when it comes to partnering with them. As we'll discuss in a later chapter, there will eventually come an opportunity with parents who are constantly living in survival mode for you and I to come alongside them and assist them.

What parents and kids want in your ministry. The way kids and their parents perceive our ministries will determine our ability to effectively partner with parents. But practically speaking, what does that mean? We need to understand what kids (and parents) are looking for and what we need to provide in order to capture their attention as we work to reach and equip them for an exciting faith journey. There are plenty of books and blogs out there that'll provide you with some insights on how to create an irresistible ministry. But for our purposes, here's a bullet list to help you evaluate your ministry environments in terms of what kids and parents are looking for.

- **Safety.** It doesn't matter whether a child is a toddler or a teenager; from a parent's perspective, safety is possibly the most important factor. A solid check-in and checkout process communicates care and professionalism to parents as they drop their kids off. While it can be frustrating for a parent to fill out registration forms with medical questions or allergy information, it also provides confidence to parents to know that their child's best interests are being looked after. Performing background checks on your volunteers and staff is also critical. Not only does it provide legal protection for your church, but knowing this has been done also gives parents another layer of security and the assurance that they're leaving their kids in good hands.

- **Relationships.** Perhaps the greatest reason children and students return week after week is because a leader has shown care and concern for them and has invested in them. Relationships eventually become the doorway to learning about God. In his book *Purpose-Driven Youth Ministry*, veteran youth worker Doug Fields reports having once heard that "until students are environmentally comfortable, they won't be theologically aware." That's so true. And establishing positive relationships with kids is a big part of making them feel comfortable.

- **Fun.** From the colors and photos on the walls to the activities, from your volunteers' attitudes to the smiles on their faces, your environment

 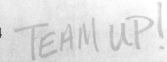

needs to communicate fun in every way. Having been in a setup and tear-down church planting environment, I know how daunting it can be to create engaging environments with few resources. But when leaders and volunteers choose to have more fun than the kids and are the first ones to let their hair down, it's amazing how much it enables the kids to relax and engage as well. With a team of excited volunteers, some fun games, and good lighting, children and students will see your environment as a fun place to learn about God.

- **Experiences.** A change that's occurring in Christian education is the movement away from lecture-based learning. Who wants to come and just be talked to? Take some extra time to allow kids to experience a lesson through active learning. It helps them learn more effectively.

- **Application.** If it doesn't apply to everyday life, it's not likely to keep kids engaged. While some theological concepts can be a little harder to grapple with, it's imperative that you find ways to help kids apply what they're learning. When it's relevant, kids will remember it and put it into practice.

- **Personal touches.** "If they don't miss me, they must not care." That's what kids and their parents think when no one follows up. Many families have entire seasons away from church. It's essential that someone takes time to follow up with those families to let them know they're missed. Simple things like sending a birthday card or a note of encouragement can make the difference in kids feeling loved and their parents feeling confident in your ministry.

Involve Parents

A common theme that I hope you see running through this book is the importance of involving parents in all that you do. Not only do parents help you get more accomplished, but they'll also become your biggest advocates and ultimately a doorway to partnering with other parents. When parents get involved, they'll treat your ministry as if it's theirs. As a result, they'll catch the biblical vision and in turn become the greatest promoters, equippers, and supporters you have of reaching the next generation for Christ.

Nearly 15 years ago I recruited Ted and his wife to help with snacks and food for the middle school ministry. Ted didn't see himself as a youth leader, but since his boys were involved, this was a good way for him to support them and their youth group. For about two years, he and his wife faithfully served food and built some great relationships with the students and other youth leaders.

The next fall we were looking to launch small groups for the first time, and it was proving hard to find good small-group leaders who loved the students and had a desire to shepherd them. With only a week to go, we had one group of seventh-grade boys who did not yet have a small-group leader. So given my limited options, we decided to ask the boys if they had any ideas. (As I said, our options were limited.) To my amazement, one of the boys instantly mentioned Ted and wanted to know if we could ask him to be their leader. Given my previous conversations with Ted, I was sure that he would instantly shoot down the idea if I asked him. But what if one of the boys asked? Genius!

Within a few days, Ted spoke to me and explained that one of the boys had asked him to be their small-group leader. "What did you say, Ted?" I asked. His reply was great. "Well, I couldn't say no to a seventh grader. So I agreed."

I wish I could tell you that Ted is still a small-group leader in the youth ministry 15 years later, but I can't. What I *can* tell you is that Ted moved from being a parent of a teen to someone who helped with the food, and then to a small-group leader and fully invested parent in the ministry for a number of years. Not only did Ted invest in those boys, but he raised the confidence of other parents and became one of our biggest advocates for the youth ministry and its vision.

Here are a few practical ideas for getting and keeping parents involved in your ministry.

- **Give them a short job description.** Having a job description for parents lets them know that you consider their role important enough to have planned and prepared for it. It will also help them to stay on track and tell when they're successfully accomplishing what you've asked them to do.
- **Share your vision and strategy with them.** When parents get involved, they become part of your team. Sharing vision and strategy helps them to know what the team is trying to accomplish and how you're trying to accomplish it. Also, once parents get involved in your ministry,

 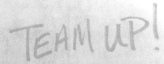

they'll often be the first ones to talk to others about its vision and strategy. It's up to you to help them know what to talk about.

- **Create entry steps for them.** Just like Ted, not all parents see themselves as leaders, but they want to help in some way. In my context some of the easiest ways for parents to get plugged in are by taking on roles such as greeters, snack providers, or setup and tear-down crewmembers. From there it's eventually possible for them to step into other leadership responsibilities such as planning events, leading small groups, or even teaching in the large-group gatherings.
- **Ensure their children are comfortable with the arrangement.** For different reasons, not every child wants his or her parents to be closely involved with the group he or she is a part of. In particular, as kids become more self-aware at the preteen age and up, there's often a desire on the part of the kids to have some distance from their parents. It's essential that parents' involvement is a win for both the parents and the kids. If you can involve a parent somewhere behind the scenes, that's often a good way to dispel the embarrassment factor that many kids feel when mom or dad is around.
- **Don't let them parent and serve at the same time.** One of the guidelines I've established for parents who lead in my ministry is that they're not allowed to discipline their own children while ministry activities are going on. If their child needs some redirection or is misbehaving, I ask the parents to get another leader to handle the situation. I set this precedent in order to avoid embarrassment for the kids. Embarrassment and shame can be a big contributor to a child not wanting to come back.

Create Family Events

As I mentioned early on in the book, there's a tendency for us as children's workers to stay focused on kids and not consider partnering with parents. In a similar way, I think we can tend to focus on kids and parents separately and not think about how we can minister to families as a whole. When that happens, we miss opportunities to bring families together in ways that enable parents and kids to continue conversations about faith at home. We also miss opportunities to help parents meet and connect with the parents of other kids in our ministries. There are times family members need to worship and learn in age-specific ways, but there's also a balance to be found in bringing parents and their children together, too.

Throughout the year our church looks for ways to bring kids and their parents together. Here are some examples of things we've done.

- **Family movie night.** Elementary-age kids and their parents came in pajamas for pizza and a fun kids' movie.
- **Parent/student rake and run.** Our students and parents went out into the community to rake leaves and do basic yardwork for single moms and widows, working quickly at each location and then moving on to the next.
- **Family crafts and carols.** Kids ages birth through elementary made crafts and sang Christmas carols for the sweet folks at a local nursing home.
- **Operation Christmas Child event.** Parents and kids worked together to buy toys, toiletries, and school supplies and pack them in shoe boxes to be sent to kids overseas through the ministry of Samaritan's Purse.
- **Family game show night.** Our middle school and high school students invited their parents to a game show night in which parents got to be the heroes (or goofs) on stage with students. Lots of laughter and fun!

There are many other great ways to hold family events that will create memories and enable families to continue their conversations at home. The previous examples are just some of the things that have worked for us. Keep in mind that it's taken us a number of years to create this many events. If you were to create just one family event this year, that's a great start. And remember to involve parents in the creation of events like these. Consider their ideas as a starting place for what will truly work. An idea that seems only average can have an incredible outcome when parents are behind it. At the same time, an incredible idea might only see an average outcome if you're trying to do it all on your own.

Schedule What Works for Parents, Not Just for You

One of the areas you and I need to be more and more strategic with is how we schedule activities and events. The prioritization of church

 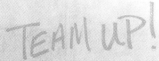

activities isn't like it used to be back in the old days when the average church family would come to Sunday morning service, Sunday evening service, and a midweek activity. (I never did that myself, but I'm told it's the way it used to be.)

The average family today has a plethora of options in any given week. Given the reality of packed schedules and extracurricular activities, it's essential to have a schedule for your ministry that's easy for parents to work into and stick with. For most children's ministries, it's easy to predict that Sunday morning services will work for parents. But what about events, parent workshops, or volunteer training times? We need to find a way to schedule those things so that we're not conflicting with parents' schedules any more than we have to. Here are some quick tips for what's helped us do that in our context.

- Survey parents to get a gauge for what days and times work best for them, and schedule events accordingly.
- Schedule well in advance, and communicate dates for special events eight to 10 weeks out.
- Don't schedule events during typically busy seasons for parents, such as the first four weeks of school, the end of school, or the beginning of summer. These are times parents will thank you for a lighter schedule.
- Try to use your facility in a way that allows you to have multiple groups meeting on campus on the same night. For example, our middle school and high school ministries meet on Wednesdays during the same time slot but in different places in the building.
- Avoid days and times that are considered to be "family times." We moved our high school ministry away from Sundays because many of our parents told us it was their only evening of the week for family time.
- For parent training events, try to have them at times parents are already on site. Don't make parents come out another night of the week when weeknights are already at a premium and parents might have to line up additional child care.

The strategies you use in your ministry serve as important steps toward seeing your vision of partnering with parents become a reality. Among other things, they build confidence and trust as parents see progress made toward the goal of reaching and equipping their kids for Christ. The strategies outlined in this chapter are only a few of the ones you'll want to include. There are likely others you can add that'll be specific to your context. Take some time to consider what strategies are most essential for you.

GAME PLAN SUMMARY

To effectively partner with parents, we must have a clear strategy for reaching and equipping kids that's easy for parents to see in action.

TEAM UP!

PRACTICE DRILLS

*Use the following action steps to help you apply
what you've learned to your life and ministry.*

1. On a scale of 1 to 5, with 1 being "No one even has their oars in" and 5 being "All oars are in and rowing in the same direction," rate your church or ministry on whether it has a synchronized team approach. Without apportioning blame to any one person or area, list some of the barriers that keep your ministry from functioning as a synchronized team. Then identify some ways you can work toward becoming a synchronized team.

2. Divide a page into two columns. On one side, list the elements that are consistent for the children and students in your ministry as they move through the age groups. On the other side, list the elements that are different from one age level to the next. Get together with a few of the key players in your children's and youth ministries, and brainstorm ways you could make the elements that are different more consistent throughout all the age groups.

3. Review this chapter for the list of things kids and parents are looking for in children's and youth ministry environments. Create a quick survey to find out how parents would rate your church or ministry in each of those areas. Assemble a group of parents and ministry leaders or volunteers to help you interpret the results of the survey. Include parents new to your ministry in this group to ensure a fresh perspective is represented.

4. Create a list of roles for parents who want to get involved in your ministry (including roles that might already be filled by parents or other volunteers). Write a basic job description for each role. Discuss the appropriate job description with those who are already serving in your ministry, affirming their value to you and the ministry and thanking them for their service. Identify parents who could fill roles that aren't currently filled, discuss with them the job description for that role, and invite them to get involved (this could include asking parents who are already serving to move into a position of greater responsibility if you think they're ready).

5. Sit down with two or three parents, and brainstorm some family events that you can do in the coming year. Choose one event to begin planning, get it onto your calendar, and ask your parent brainstorming team to help you make it happen.

6. Evaluate your ministry calendar in terms of how you think it adds to or alleviates stress in parents' schedules. Look at the list of scheduling tips within this chapter. Choose one you think is especially helpful, and apply it to your calendar.

TEAM UP!

Chapter 9

POINT TO
IMPORTANT
MILESTONES

*How to help parents
and kids know they're
heading down the right road.*

Shortly after I graduated from high school, I took a road trip with my good friend Martin. We had much in common, such as our love of soccer and music, but we also shared a similar faith journey. Both of us grew up outside the church and were invited by friends to the same local youth group. Martin and I came to Christ at the same time and were baptized on the same day. But when we graduated from high school, he went off to university while I stayed home and worked. It was a tough time for me personally, since I felt like most of my good friends—like Martin—had left for an exciting life at college while I worked in a boring accounts department.

I'm an extrovert. And accounting is an extrovert's nightmare. I hate numbers and love people. Anytime I could get away to catch up with my friends, I'd jump in my rusty Ford Fiesta for a road trip. (I love taking road trips, too!) Once while Martin was home on winter break, he asked if I could drive him back to his university to pick up some important books he needed over the break. It was a great opportunity to hang out with

Martin and get to see his new life at school. So we set off on a cold January morning with our destination in sight…or so I thought.

It took us about two hours to navigate around the M25, which is a circular freeway that circumvents the whole city of London. (At rush hour, I like to call it the largest circular parking lot in the world.) We were excited when we saw signs for the exit leading us to Reading University, where Martin went to school. I'd never been to the city of Reading before, but of course Martin had been there many times by now. I had no reason to doubt his navigation, and I was sure that the next part of our journey would be a whole lot easier than the crawl of the M25.

Before long we were heading up the M40 motorway, enjoying each other's company and the rolling hills of the English countryside. About an hour later, I began to see snow on top of the hills and more and more sheep around us. While I loved looking at the rolling hills of England, I didn't like what the snow and sheep indicated about the direction we were heading. It was the road sign telling us that Birmingham was only 80 miles away that made us realize we were indeed heading in the wrong direction. Reading is due west of London. Seeing signs for Birmingham told us we were clearly heading northwest. It wasn't long before we came to discover what the problem was: Reading is just off the M4 motorway, not the M40. (If only we would've had a GPS back then.)

While Martin and I had a destination in mind, we didn't have a map to help us evaluate our progress on the journey. I knew that Birmingham wasn't near Reading, but we still traveled a long way up the freeway admiring the snow-covered hills and sheep when we could have already been at our destination. In a similar way, parents often know where their kids need to get to in their faith journeys and have every intention of helping them get there, but they don't always know what to look for to help their kids confirm they're on the right path.

Why Milestones Are Important

In Chapter 4 we talked about the importance of casting for parents the biblical vision for raising their children with a strong faith foundation. Casting such a vision helps parents see the big picture of the faith journey their children are on, like showing them the destination on a road map.

TEAM UP!

However, it's also important that we help parents identify the particular routes their children need to take to get to that destination, marking out where and what direction their kids need to turn to be successful on their journeys. We do that in part by helping them to see the crucial milestones to watch for. If a clear biblical vision is a destination for parents to head toward, milestones serve as strategic markers along the way.

In his book *Shift—What It Takes to Finally Reach Families Today,* Brian Haynes talks about the milestones his church focuses on, saying:

> "These milestones serve as markers of progression on the spiritual formation journey. When a person reaches a milestone, that growth is celebrated as a praise for how God is working in the person and as a motivation to continue walking the path."

That's a great description of what milestones are and how to best interact with them.

Without milestones, many parents end up sending their kids on a journey in the wrong direction without realizing it. Their kids experience a lot of good things along the way, but they're also ill-equipped for the long haul ahead. The parents you and I will meet will often have the right intentions for their children but will also be taking them in the wrong direction, missing crucial milestones along the way. I can't tell you how many parents I meet who look back and see many missed opportunities to intentionally invest in their child's faith journey. Most of them sincerely care about their kids and wanted to help them become successful in life and faith. However, in their attempt to raise well-rounded, successful kids, they got swept along in a tide of extracurricular activities and missed opportunities to bring faith into focus and incorporate faith into everyday life.

Parents may be in the driver's seat, but we can't assume they always know where they're heading or how to get there. As quickly as they hear and agree with the vision to raise their kids with a solid faith foundation, they're back to their day-to-day journeys of parenting in survival mode. Instead of becoming annoying "back-seat drivers," we need to come alongside parents as helpful navigators. We need to point them to crucial milestones that'll help them keep their kids on track to developing a solid faith foundation.

Focus on What Matters Most

Not all milestones look the same. The milestones you point parents toward will depend in part on the denominational background you're a part of. My journey of faith and ministry has taken me on a varied denominational path that's enabled me to understand and appreciate the unique qualities of a number of denominations. I've had the privilege of attending or ministering in Anglican, Baptist, Lutheran, Evangelical Covenant, Wesleyan, and nondenominational churches. (If I missed your denomination, don't worry; it seems as though I'm working my way toward it at some point.) My wife's family is Roman Catholic, and I'm well connected with friends who are in ministry roles in all kinds of denominational backgrounds. As you'd expect, I do have my doctrinal convictions. But I also love the theological diversity that can be found in the church today.

That being said, you might not agree with all the milestones I'm suggesting. But it's essential that you apply the principle of helping parents identify important milestones in your context. Don't get hung up on whether you agree with the particular milestones themselves. Rather, consider your unique denominational identity, and look for milestones that parents in your ministry can easily follow and apply in their family situations.

How to Incorporate Milestones in Your Ministry

Earlier I mentioned Brian Haynes' book *Shift—What It Takes to Finally Reach Families Today*. In it he outlines a number of steps that his church takes with parents in their milestones strategy. The items in the following list are adapted from the steps Haynes has identified, and they offer three basic ideas for incorporating an emphasis on milestones in your ministry.

- **Core Teaching** For every milestone, provide parents (and their children) with a practical and biblical teaching that focuses on: (1) The significance of the milestone, (2) how God has been faithful and present up until now, and (3) preparation for the next part of the child's journey. This can be offered in a formal class, a booklet, or as a handout.

- **Cues for Parents** To reinforce the teaching, give parents a number of ways to continue the conversation at home with their kids. These can include conversation starters and activities that focus again on the significance of the milestone, God's presence and faithfulness, and preparation for the next steps.
- **Celebration** Whether it's a church event or something parents create for their child at home, celebrate each milestone when the child reaches it. This could involve anything from a dinner at the child's favorite restaurant to a father/son or mother/daughter getaway. Suggest ideas to parents such as writing a letter to their child or giving the child a gift that's symbolic of the particular milestone he or she has reached as a way to emphasize its significance.

There are many more things you and I could do to implement effective milestones, but it's important to take one step at a time. Not only are your parents and kids on a journey of faith that requires them to take one step at a time, but we also must not forget that implementing milestones might require you take one step at a time. When I first started to consider what I could do to point parents to milestones, I wanted to change the world all at once. I wanted to create parent seminars for each milestone, and I had ideas for all kinds of elaborate celebrations for parents and kids. However, I've learned (and am learning) that it's better to implement a few simple ideas, get them established and sustainable, and then move on to something more. So often there's a tendency to want to do it all at once. But that's not sustainable for us, and it's not likely to be implemented well.

One thing I have found to be helpful is to work with parents to create a "map" of the journey they and their kids are on with the essential milestones marked along the way. It can be a one-page sheet that looks like an actual road map (if you're the creative type) or something as simple as a chart or list of key milestones. Creating a map can be a helpful way for you and them to visualize the journey they're on, especially as they consider the next steps that are coming along. Including a specific destination is perhaps the most important part of such a map, helping parents identify who they want their children to become. That destination will ultimately dictate the direction parents guide their kids and influence their level of determination to watch for the critical milestones.

Other elements to include in a map of milestones are:

- The name of each milestone from pre-birth to adulthood;
- A one-sentence description of the milestone's significance;
- Space for parents to write a one-sentence, developmental description of the child at each milestone (where the child's development was for milestones that have already passed or where they hope the child's development will be for milestones yet to come);
- Space for parents to describe how God was present and faithful up to that point (for milestones the child has already reached);
- A one-sentence description of what's ahead for the child and how he or she can begin preparing for the next milestone to come.

Critical Milestones

Moses' words in Deuteronomy 6:4-9 provided the people of Israel a road map for incorporating faith into everyday living. He encouraged parents to communicate faith to their children in the teachable moments of everyday living and also by creating intentional faith traditions that would help their children remember the commandments God had given. Those are the same things we want to encourage parents to do when we point them to important milestones. With that in mind, let's look at two specific types of milestones that are significant in the lives of parents and their children: faith milestones and life milestones.

Faith milestones are rooted in biblical tradition and focus. They point to commitment and deepening faith steps that children or their parents will take on their faith journeys. They also celebrate and point to all that God is doing and has done in the life of a child and his or her family. Depending on your denominational background, faith milestones could include (but are not limited to) things such as dedication, salvation, communion, baptism, or confirmation. While these milestones aren't directly connected to the different life milestones we'll look at later, faith in general—to which these milestones point—has a significant overlap with and influence on those other milestones. That's why I've mentioned them first. As most denominations provide their own teaching on these kinds of milestones, along with a format for celebrating those that they practice, much of what you need to incorporate faith milestones into your ministry may already be in place.

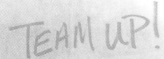

Life milestones are turning points that occur naturally and normally in the daily, weekly, monthly, and yearly activities of parents and their kids. For many parents and children, these natural and normal turning points often offer little or no acknowledgment of what God has done or is doing. It's our job to help parents take specific and strategic steps to create milestones that celebrate what God has done and invite him into the next phase of the journey. Usually these are times that every child or adult will look back on as defining moments in their lives. From starting school to entering adulthood, there are certain turning points in life where we all need to put a stake in the ground, acknowledging God's work thus far and looking forward to the journey ahead with him.

The following is a list of six life milestones that I would suggest—and you are welcome to add others. The key is finding significant turning points in the life of a child or parent and then including faith into those times.

Birth It's definitely a milestone when a child is conceived and parents start looking forward to the child's birth. Consider the amount of time and resources first-time parents pour into preparing for the arrival of their child. At this stage they're typically very focused and determined to do whatever it takes to set their child up for success. It's not that parents don't care when second and third children come along. The first child just provides a greater degree of first-time learning and experience. Just consider the amount of time, energy, and money that goes into decorating the baby's room and buying the cutest clothes for a first child. Consider the amount of reading and education a first-time parent is willing to invest in. I still remember reluctantly attending a birth class with Lisa for a couple of weeks and reading a book for guys about being a new father. (I remember that it had just enough macho stories to keep me interested.) The fact is, a first-time parent is more receptive to learning new things than at any other time.

The reality for us in ministry is that the church has more opportunity to speak into the lives of expecting parents than at any other time of the parenting journey. So often we begin conversations about faith formation after the baby is born when the parents are exhausted and already on the path to survival mode. Meeting with and investing in parents who are expecting their first child is perhaps the best opportunity to help them create a faith map with strategic milestones. In some respects it's like mapping out a journey prior to getting in the car and heading off down the road. It's so much better to figure out the routes and milestones before the journey starts than to get lost in the winding roads and fog of parenting not knowing how to get back on track.

The start of school The first day of school is always a big deal. It can be scary and exciting all at the same time. There's a flurry of activity around shopping for new clothes and school supplies and getting kids a new haircut so they look good for their big first day. There are also the anxieties kids and parents can experience: for kids, the uncertainty that comes with new teachers, new classrooms, or even new classmates; for parents, the fretfulness of wanting their kids to succeed but knowing they're losing a measure of control. At this significant turning point in the life of a child (and his or her parents), creating a milestone is a powerful way to remind them both of how God has been with them and helped them in the past and that he will continue to be with them in the years ahead.

Puberty I currently sit on a reproductive health committee for my local school system. It's composed of parents, teachers, community leaders, and a solitary pastor (that's me). Part of our role is to oversee what curriculum makes it into the classroom and at what ages kids are deemed ready to receive certain aspects of sex education. What I really appreciate about this committee is its focus on partnering with parents and allowing parents to be the ones who share vital information with their kids. My experience on this committee has made me even more committed to assist and support parents as they reach this milestone, celebrating the changes in their child's life while also giving them a healthy road map for their relationships now and in the future.

For most parents, talking about sexuality and relationships can be very awkward and unnerving. However, there's too much at stake for parents not to have these conversations. Given the choice of allowing culture to dictate their child's view on sexuality or having that talk themselves, most parents will choose to get over their apprehensions. In a world that's increasingly over-sexualized, it's essential that we empower and equip parents to help their kids discover God's best for sex and relationships. When we provide parents with resources and helpful teaching on the topic, it has a positive effect on their kids' lives.

TEAM UP!

Adolescence Let me just say it: Adolescence is messy! Having spent over 20 years in youth ministry, I can attest to the confusion and struggle that both parents and students go through in this precarious time of life. I can also attest to the relief both parties experience when they turn the corner out of adolescence and look back to see how God has helped them navigate the joys and the challenges in this season of life. I compare adolescence to traveling down a winding country lane in England on a foggy day. You never know what's coming around the corner, and the direction seems to be ever-changing from one moment to the next. Therefore, given what children and parents are about to enter into as they encounter adolescence, it's essential that we help them develop some realistic expectations and helpful tools for the journey ahead.

Graduation Growing up in England meant that I never saw a great deal of celebration for this life milestone. While it's changed a bit in recent years, most kids in the U.K. don't have a graduation party or receive cards or gifts from family and friends. Perhaps it's because we Brits are too focused on the end of the soccer season at that time of year. Regardless of what my fellow Brits do, I know that here in the United

HELPING GRADUATES CELEBRATE

Here are some additional things your church can do to make a graduation Sunday especially meaningful for students and their parents.

- Give graduating students a gift with a practical and spiritual emphasis such as a Bible, a devotional book, or spiritually uplifting music.

- Have parents write a letter to their graduating students to affirm their accomplishment, and offer to let them read it during the service.

- Let students display a photo collage for church members to look at before and after the service.

- Pair students and their parents with a prayer partner at church—someone who will check in with and pray for the student and family regularly.

- Have a photographer take photos of students with their parents, small-group leaders, and church staff where applicable, and send the pictures to the family.

- Invite a youth ministry volunteer or a prominent church leader to pray for graduating students during the service.

- Commission students to minister wherever the next season of life is taking them (college, the military, the workforce, etc.).

States graduation is a big deal. And given that students and parents place such a big emphasis on congratulating and celebrating, it's important that we help them to bring a spiritual emphasis to the celebration. By doing so we enable them to give God the glory and to look ahead as they continue their journey with their heavenly father.

Many churches set aside a Sunday to celebrate their high school graduates. In the past few years, I've asked to preach in the main service that day, and I've created a sermon that's relevant to graduates and also applicable to everyone else. It's another way I've used to focus on the significance of this milestone, to emphasize how God has been present and faithful, and to prepare graduating students (and their parents) for the next part of the journey. It's also a great way to encourage church members to support parents and students as they transition into a new season of life.

Adulthood It's now thought by some that adolescence isn't complete until individuals reach their mid-20s, which could explain why adulthood can feel as if it's a long way off for some students. Whether that's true or not, the transition to adulthood doesn't necessarily correspond with graduation from high school. For some it can come later; for others it can come sooner. Developmentally, most students will not have fully attained the status of adult. (My wife maintains that I have yet to attain this myself.) But it's essential to provide some strategic steps to help students enter into this next stage of their lives regardless of their age.

For the past five years, my family has headed to West Michigan for our summer vacation. Not only do we love the beaches of Lake Michigan, but we also love to see our good friends Troy and Amy. We usually end up hanging out with them at our favorite beach, having a blast swimming with the kids while my pasty English skin gets sunburned. Troy has a humble wisdom that's been developed from an authentic faith walk. I always love spending time listening to him and gaining insight from what he has to say.

Recently both of Troy's teenage boys were getting ready to head off to college, leaving Amy and him to be empty nesters. But before his boys left for college, Troy wanted to create a milestone for them that would be etched in their memories for many years to come. Months prior he asked his boys to write down the names of Christian men who had influenced their lives, what about each of those men had influenced them, and how

TEAM UP!

they saw Christ in each of those men. Without the boys knowing it, he sent their notes to the men they identified and invited each of them to a dinner where they would pray for the boys, share their collective wisdom, and give them God-honoring advice for the future.

One summer evening the boys arrived at a beautiful house overlooking Lake Michigan, having been told only to dress up a little and to come hungry. When they arrived, they were blown away to see the men whose names they had written down and talked with Troy about just a few months previously. After dinner, a time of sharing, and a time of prayer, Troy's sons were each presented with a large, wood-framed mirror that was engraved on the outside with some words to remind them in the years to come that they were men of God, called to walk steadfastly in the faith and to reflect Christ to everyone. Troy's sons arrived at that house as boys on a journey. But once they encountered this milestone, they were ready to move into adulthood as young Christian men, commissioned by their father and a group of godly men.

Troy's idea has been emulated many times by his friends. It would be a great way for parents you know to help their kids step into adulthood, too. Or perhaps you might even use it yourself.

Other Milestones

In speaking with friends of mine who are in ministry, I've come across some other areas that are helpful to have milestones created around. The following ideas don't lend themselves to merging life and faith as easily. But it's crucial to see these life issues as areas in which children and students greatly need the kind of direction that comes from experiencing a milestone event. Anytime a parent can apply faith to these issues is an opportunity to make faith stick in a greater way.

Media Milestones Kids are getting into technology at a younger age and are exposed to more and more in the media all the time. If parents aren't careful to create some kind of media milestone for their kids, it's very possible that at some point they'll all pay the price. An example of creating a milestone around the use of media and technology would be having kids sign a media contract. A media contract defines the terms of appropriate technology usage and enables parents to come alongside their children and talk about wise decisions, guarding their hearts, and moderation. It also enables parents to call their kids to a greater level of responsibility in their lives.

Driving Milestones What teenager can't wait to drive? All right, there might be a few who prefer riding horseback. But most kids can't wait for the day they get their driver's license. It's a bit of a milestone in itself. Parents can add to the significance of the event by coming alongside their child with something like a parent-teen driving agreement. As with a media contract, a driving agreement gives parents an opportunity to talk with their children about wise decisions and challenges students with an even greater sense of responsibility. Organizations such as the Centers for Disease Control and Prevention (cdc.gov) have printable driving agreements parents can use or adapt to include elements of faith.

Money Milestones Once students have the ability to make their own money, it's a great time for parents to create a milestone event that allows them to come alongside their kids and talk about financial responsibility. As students take a step toward adulthood and greater independence, parents can support and equip them with some basic biblical principles for managing money, such as tithing, saving, and spending wisely. One idea for doing this is for parents to let their child earn money by working around the home in some way. The work should be separate from the child's normal chores, and the amount earned should be separate from any regular allowance he or she receives. When the work is done and the child has been paid, the parents and child can set up a time to go out and spend the money under the following guidelines: The child has to give 10 percent of what he or she has earned to the church first, save 10 percent, and spend at least part of what's left on someone else, perhaps buying something for a sibling or a friend. Then the parents could celebrate with their child by taking him or her out for a meal at a favorite restaurant (or even out for just an ice cream cone if that's all the parents' finances will allow).

Make Milestones Stand Out

Years ago before we had kids, Lisa and I backpacked around Europe one summer. (Did I tell you that I love to travel?) One of our favorite countries to visit was Ireland. There's just something about the Emerald Isle that's wonderful and relaxing. It was also quite an adventure driving

on the country roads. We nearly ran over several sheep and sheepdogs along the way, and I'm surprised we didn't get lost more often than we did. You see, in that part of the country, road signs, markers, and milestones aren't really designed to stand out. They just sort of blend into the surroundings. (When we arrived back in the States, it was like the road signs were shouting at us.) If not for my highly trained and observant navigator—Lisa—we would've been perpetually lost.

Milestones in the faith journey of a child should be a big deal. They should be monuments children and parents create together to celebrate all that God has done and to look forward to all he will do. Anytime you and I can help parents provide directions and navigational markers for their child, it'll be a defining moment for both of them.

GAME PLAN SUMMARY

By pointing parents to milestones in their kids' lives, we help both of them evaluate where they are now and whether they're on track to get where they want to go.

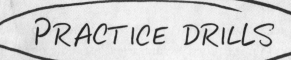

PRACTICE DRILLS

*Use the following action steps to help you apply
what you've learned to your life and ministry.*

1. Take some time to journal about the milestones you've experienced in your own life. In what ways were your parents involved in those milestones? What lessons from your experiences with milestones could help you point out milestones parents should be watching for in their kids' lives?

2. Create a list of the milestones your church helps kids and parents celebrate, including both faith and life milestones. What milestones could you add to this list in the future?

3. Choose one milestone to start pointing parents to right away. Begin developing a core teaching, some parent cues, and a celebration to help parents highlight that milestone in their child's life.

4. Create a "map" of the journey parents and their kids are on, marking significant milestones along the way from birth through adulthood. You might also recruit an artistically gifted parent to create a pictorial version of your map. Regardless of the form your map takes, leave space for parents to add in notes about their child's development at each milestone and ways God has been present and faithful.

TEAM UP!

Chapter 10

HELP OUT IN **HARD TIMES**

How helping families in difficulty opens the door for partnering with parents.

Claire's* baby wasn't supposed to make it. About halfway through the pregnancy, Claire received the devastating news that her baby had an extremely rare chromosomal disorder that would likely result in the baby not making it to full term. There had only been a handful of documented cases of this disorder. And in the unlikely event that the baby did make it to full term, there had been only two babies with the disorder who had survived. It was extremely difficult news to comprehend. And it was painfully hard to explain to her elementary-age daughter, who was elated about becoming a big sister. Claire had been away from church for a while, and Lisa and I didn't know her and her daughter that well. But we felt compelled to come alongside her and see what we could do to help her through this gut-wrenching time.

The weeks passed quickly, and it seemed as if the baby was making fairly normal progress. It was also amazing to see how God was giving Claire strength and comfort each day despite the great uncertainty that lay ahead. It wasn't long before the doctors planned to induce labor in the hope they could give the baby a greater chance of survival. With all that I knew about the situation, the pessimist in me didn't expect the baby to make it through the birth. I was already thinking about how to best comfort the family. But in that time, I also sensed God redirecting my energy to pray for a miracle and for this little baby to live.

To everyone's amazement and joy, Claire had a beautiful baby girl who's now one of only three babies with this condition to survive past birth. When Lisa and I arrived at the hospital to meet this little miracle, it was wonderful to see Claire with a beaming smile, full of God-given confidence. Her little girl will have many special needs in her lifetime. But it's been wonderful to be a part of their journey in the past year and to help Claire and her older daughter find hope and support in our church family.

Just a few weeks after the baby was born, our church had an incredible weeklong camp for elementary-age kids that I thought Claire's older daughter would love. When I didn't see her name on the registration list, however, I wasn't surprised. I knew Claire was living in survival mode. She was receiving meals from the church, and various family and friends were supporting her. All this was entirely new territory for her, and every minute of her day was occupied with doctors' visits, caring for a baby with special needs, and looking after her eldest. Eventually I was able to make contact. I got her older daughter registered for the camp and invited Claire to come to coffee time every morning for the moms of the campers. I didn't expect her to have time, but I hoped we could get her better connected with some of the great women at our church. To my amazement, she came every day. It was during that time that she had some great conversations, including one with another mom who had a child with special needs.

Claire is now in a Bible study for moms of children with special needs. That's where she experiences the love and support of a group of women who understand and care for her. These days Lisa and I see her every week at church, and she often stops by our home with her little miracle to hang out with Lisa while her older daughter has play dates with one of our kids.

Lessons From Helping Hurting Parents

One of the most significant ways you and I can begin to partner with parents is to support them in hard times. There are parents in our ministries who—like Claire—are going through challenging times and feel alone in their predicament. Their circumstances may not be as dramatic as Claire's,

but they're difficult nonetheless. When we seize the opportunity to come alongside these parents, it not only meets their need in the moment, but it can open the door to supporting and equipping them in other ways in the future.

While every situation is different, let me share some helpful lessons from my experience with helping Claire and other parents like her. As you navigate through these points, be thinking and praying about specific parents in your ministry you could support in greater ways.

Be attentive. Coming alongside parents when they're facing difficult situations requires us to be alert to what's going on in their lives and to be intentional about offering them support. The challenge for many of us is that we're sometimes too focused on our programs to be aware of the people around us. Consequently, we don't always do very well with offering support either. On the other hand, many parents do a good job of hiding their struggles. They come to church and drop their kids off with what I refer to as fake church smiles. They offer a cordial "good morning" or "hello," but there can be a lot more going on inside. Not every situation is as complex and unique as Claire's, but you can be sure that every family you come into contact with is navigating its own challenging situations at times. It's essential that you and I are as attentive as possible and recognize those challenging situations as God-given opportunities to come alongside parents and partner with them.

Communicate with your team. It's impossible for one person to see all the needs of the families that come to your church. That's why it's so important to have a system of communication that ensures you and your team (staff and volunteers) can share with each other what you're seeing. There are times I would be completely unaware of a hardship a family is facing unless another staff member was able to clue me in on it.

My team's system for communicating the needs we see involves taking a few minutes in our weekly meetings to share any concerns or prayer requests that we have for families facing adversity. Then we're also able to discuss what would be the appropriate ways for us to assist in those situations.

With all that in mind, it's also imperative that each person on your team understands the expectation of maintaining confidentiality regarding those things that are shared. Don't let the communication of information within your team become a source of gossip or embarrassment to the families you minister to.

Work with others. Just as it's impossible to know all that's occurring in the life of a family, it's also impossible for one person to attend to every need. It's necessary that we all take a team approach and spread out the load of care and support. In the case of Claire, our care ministries director was able to orchestrate meeting her practical needs and our small-groups coordinator focused on getting her connected with the moms' Bible study. I was able to get her connected with other parents by lining up play dates for her older daughter in addition to the time they spent with Lisa and our kids. Over the past year or so, there have been four or more people who've played a key role in seeing Claire get connected, find support, and grow deeper in her relationship with God. And her two kids are benefiting from a mom who feels hopeful about the future and is making faith a huge priority these days.

Connect parents with experts. In the chapter on providing resources to parents, we talked about how crucial it is to develop a list of experts in your church or community who can help parents and their kids. Knowing the names of some good counselors, doctors, or other professionals with expertise on children and the family will be something for which parents facing hard times will be forever thankful.

There are a lot of parents who'll never allow you into their lives while they're living life in the fast lane and their kids are doing reasonably well. However, there will often be opportunities where parents or their kids find themselves lost on the highway of life and in need of help and support. It's in these moments that an attentive and caring person like you or me can come alongside them and make a real difference. Seizing those opportunities will not only help them deal with whatever pain they're experiencing at that time, but it could also open doors to continue partnering with them on their journeys down the road.

GAME PLAN SUMMARY

Seizing the opportunity to help parents facing hard times can become an entry point to partnering with them in their parenting journeys.

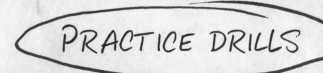

PRACTICE DRILLS

*Use the following action steps to help you apply
what you've learned to your life and ministry.*

1. List your top barriers to being aware of difficulties in the lives of the families to whom you minister. Brainstorm some ways you can overcome those barriers, and choose one of those ways to put into practice.

2. At your next regular ministry team meeting, ask "Which families in our congregation are struggling or experiencing some kind of pain?" Then discuss appropriate ways to offer help or comfort to the families that are mentioned. Assign members of your team to lead the efforts in helping each family mentioned.

3. Write down the primary ways in which you and your team communicate when a family hardship arises in your church. Meet with your team, and discuss ways you could improve communication to ensure that you're not missing opportunities to assist and support parents in need.

4. Create a list of people in your church who could provide practical, spiritual, and emotional support to parents. Contact those people, and ask their permission to give their names out as necessary to parents you think they could offer help.

5. Familiarize yourself with the family support options available through your church. Ask the person who oversees the congregational care of your church (this could be your pastor, a staff member, or a volunteer) to share with you his or her process for caring for families dealing with difficult circumstances.

TEAM UP!

Chapter 11

BUILD A
NETWORK OF
PARTNERS

*The importance of connecting
parents with others who can
partner with them as well.*

A number of years ago I sat down in a Starbucks with youth ministry veteran Mark DeVries after hearing him speak at a local university. (I was following the example of my youth ministry mentor Byron Porisch by networking with and learning from some of the leaders in the field of ministry.) Mark is a fascinating leader with innovative ideas. While in the trenches of ministry, he'd written a number of books. He'd also written a number of articles I'd read about family ministry and how to involve the whole church in investing in the life of a child. As we sat in that coffeehouse, Mark drew on a napkin a plan for creating a web of support for every child and student in a given church. The premise of the diagram was for children's and youth ministry workers to see themselves as networkers within their local churches, connecting children and students to a wide variety of people who could pour into their lives.

As workers in children's and youth ministry, there's a tendency for us to see our roles purely as creators of great environments for kids. However, one of the things that's missing when we do that is the opportunity for kids and students to feel a sense of belonging and connection with the church as a whole. As a leader I've come to realize that I can't be there for every person at every moment. But just as a sports team works to develop a "deep bench" with as many high-level players as possible at every position, connecting kids with a wide range of adults provides them with a deep bench of people who can offer them support in the moments when they need it most. As Mark DeVries told me, "There are no more Lone Rangers." And he encouraged me to create a culture in my church where kids would have multiple people surrounding them, forming a web of support so they'd have someone to call on whenever they needed to. This is one of the first and most crucial steps in creating a healthy family ministry that envisions the whole church supporting and equipping the next generation—not just those serving in the children's or youth ministries.

Over time it had become part of my focus to create webs of support for the next generation by connecting kids with all kinds of people in the local church. But for many years I missed the fact that kids weren't the only ones who needed that kind of support. Their parents needed it, too. One day I began to ask what would happen if parents were better supported in raising their kids in the faith. I wondered how kids would be affected if that were to happen. And that started me thinking about the people in my church whom parents needed to be connected with as avenues for help and support and how I could create a better network to connect parents with those people.

Parents Need to Know They're Not Alone

When Gavin and Wendy* had their first child, they were full of joy and love for the little blessing that had been given to them. Like so many young couples, they also quickly realized their schedule was no longer their own. That became an even stronger reality by the time they'd had their third child. But they would always maintain, "We wouldn't change this for the world!" With big church smiles planted on their faces, they'd rush their kids through check-in and make it into the service just as the music was ending.

While Gavin and Wendy felt blessed by their kids and their life as parents, it wasn't long until the cracks began to show. The realities of their new schedule meant that small group, quality friendships, and margin in

 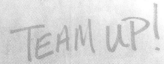

their lives had taken a back seat for many years. One evening after a run of sleepless nights and the usual parenting challenges, Wendy asked Gavin:

> "How do we know if we're getting it right? Everyone else seems to have it all together with their kids. I have a teenager who doesn't talk to me anymore, a preteen who's overly emotional, and a toddler who's defiant every day. I love my kids, but how do I know if I'm getting it right?"

Having three kids of my own, I can relate to Gavin and Wendy in so many ways. Having kids is a huge blessing and privilege. But there are seasons I feel tired and overwhelmed. It's during these times that Lisa and I need to know we're not alone and that we can count on good advice and support from others. Sadly, many parents don't have that kind of support.

Help Parents Develop a Web of Support

In a world in which people move frequently, it's often hard to know where to find good help. Add in a church culture that sometimes lacks authenticity—with people showing up looking as if they have it all together—and no wonder it's a challenge for parents to reach out for help. For those of us in ministry, you can add on the unspoken expectation that somehow being in ministry automatically qualifies us to be great parents. (If only that were true...but it's not.) There have been times Lisa and I have felt isolated and alone in our parenting journey because we didn't feel we could admit our failings to anyone else.

All parents need a web of support to help them on their parenting journey. It's important for them to be surrounded by people who can help and encourage them as they raise their kids. As with so many things in life, there's no manual with all the answers for questions parents will ask. But God often provides other people who can act as resources for those who need help. So even if you're not a parent yourself, it's imperative that you understand your role in connecting parents with a network they can rely on as they invest in their kids.

Let's take a look at some ways you and I can help parents develop that kind of network.

Practice radical hospitality. The first step in building a web of support for parents is to create a culture where parents can feel free to show up as they are. In their book *Why Nobody Wants to Go to Church Anymore*, Thom and Joani Schultz talk about the importance of practicing radical hospitality, which includes authentically welcoming people and accepting them no matter what. Most parents carry a degree of insecurity about their parenting. And sadly, many have felt judged by the church in the past. Though I've often practiced radical hospitality with the kids and students in my ministry, I know there are also many times I haven't practiced it well with parents. We need to ensure that every parent in our ministry receives the message to "come as you are." They need to know they're not being judged and that there are others who understand what it's like to be imperfect at parenting. We need to go the extra mile to help parents feel welcome and accepted.

Connect parents with other parents. As I've mentioned in previous chapters, it's essential to connect parents with other parents in your ministry. Many parents feel as though they're the only ones who make mistakes or have kids with problems. But the truth is, once parents sit down and begin to share stories with each other, it doesn't take long for them to realize that they aren't really any different from everyone else. Part of our responsibility is to connect parents with one another so they can find that kind of support in a community of faith.

Recruit seasoned parents. Parents with kids still at home need to know they're not alone and that there are others who've successfully gone before them. Some of the best partners you can have for your ministry are empty nesters who've "been there, done that, and got the T-shirt." Recently I had one couple approach me about helping out in just this way. They told me:

> "When we were parents with kids at home, we often wondered if we were getting it right. Fortunately, we had a lot of support from some great people who were a few years ahead of us. Now we want to do the same for other parents. How can we help?"

I don't get parents like this coming to me every day. But getting experienced parents involved doesn't usually take much. I've never had a parent whose kids are grown tell me no when asked to come alongside a younger

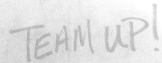

parent. Those who've navigated through the parenting journey know just how important it is to have support along the way. There are plenty of experienced parents in your church who can make an eternal difference in the lives of the parents and kids currently in your ministry. Once you've recruited one or two parents, they can help you recruit others.

Promote small groups. Practically speaking, one of the best things we can do for parents is encourage them to be part of a small group or Bible study—especially if it means they'll be able to gather with other parents. We need to be huge cheerleaders of these types of ministries. When parents become invested in a small group or Bible study, they'll not only begin to experience authentic community, but they'll also deepen in their faith. When that happens, there'll be a positive effect on how they function in their roles as parents.

Strengthen the connection between parents and volunteers. Effective children's and youth ministry volunteers not only invest in kids' lives, they understand and respond to the needs of parents, too. In my ministry there are several steps we take to help volunteers reach out to parents and also make it easy for parents to get in contact with the volunteers who are investing in their children. For example, all our small-group leaders are provided with a profile card they can give to parents containing the leaders' pictures, a few sentences about themselves, and their contact information. Leaders are also trained and encouraged to make contact with parents at least once a semester (though some do it more). And every year we host a ministry open house that allows parents to experience the ministry environments their kids participate in and to meet with their child's small-group leaders.

In a previous church, Marve and Holly were two of my most faithful youth volunteers. They were empty nesters, had loads of time, and never seemed to run out of energy. The students loved them, and the parents did, too. Given that their kids had all grown up and left the house, they had an amazing opportunity to encourage and support parents who were still trudging through the challenges of raising teenagers. Marve and Holly are not only great examples of how experienced parents can support parents who are still in the trenches, but they also show the importance of connecting parents and volunteers as well. Parents grew to trust them and felt as though they were true partners with parents in raising their kids in the faith. Volunteers don't have to be experienced parents like Marve and Holly were, but they can still become a trusted source of encouragement and support to parents when the appropriate connections are made.

Many of the parents you and I minister to are working as hard as they can to give their kids the best things they can. But they're also feeling as though they're going it alone, struggling to know the best way to help their kids. God didn't make any of us to operate in isolation. He designed us for community and to be a support to one another. That's true for you and me, and it's true for the parents in our churches and communities. The challenge is for us to see ourselves as networkers, connecting parents to those who can give them the vital support and encouragement they need as they navigate through the parenting years.

GAME PLAN SUMMARY

Partnering with parents includes helping them connect with others in your church who can offer them encouragement and support.

TEAM UP!

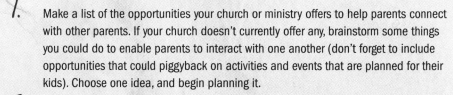

PRACTICE DRILLS

*Use the following action steps to help you apply
what you've learned to your life and ministry.*

1. Make a list of the opportunities your church or ministry offers to help parents connect with other parents. If your church doesn't currently offer any, brainstorm some things you could do to enable parents to interact with one another (don't forget to include opportunities that could piggyback on activities and events that are planned for their kids). Choose one idea, and begin planning it.

2. On a scale of 1 to 5, with 1 being "Come in if you must" and 5 being "We're excited you're here," grade your ministry on how well you practice radical hospitality (authentically welcoming parents and accepting them no matter what). What grade do you think the parents you minister to would give you? What are some steps your ministry could take to improve in this area?

3. Create a list of parents in your church who have a reputation of being God-honoring and whose children are grown. Contact them, and ask if they'd be available to come alongside parents whose kids are still at home to offer them encouragement and support.

4. Hold an open house for your ministry that enables parents to see the environments their kids participate in and to meet their kids' volunteer leaders. Provide your volunteers information cards they can give to parents that include the volunteers' names, pictures, a few sentences about themselves, and their contact information.

WHAT'S AT STAKE?

"**A**fter that generation died, another generation grew up who did not acknowledge the Lord or remember the mighty things he had done for Israel" (Judges 2:10). That verse has often made me pause and reflect on the importance of what I do. A whole generation had followed Joshua, and yet the generation that came after them was completely lost. Somewhere along the way, that first generation of people failed to pass down their faith to their children. It's as though they'd forgotten the words that Moses had spoken in Deuteronomy 6:4-9.

Depending on what study you read, it appears that droves of kids today are walking away from their faith despite having been involved in the church for most of their lives. Even though they've walked through the doors of children's and student ministries week after week, many of them are still deciding to exit their faith journey at graduation. The kids in our ministries will one day grow up to graduate from high school and head off to work or college whether they've developed a solid faith foundation or not. And while our ministries certainly have something to do with whether that faith foundation is developed, we have to embrace the reality that what we do is only a part of God's blueprint for passing the faith on to kids. If we want to see children and students develop the best faith foundation they can, we have to partner with parents and help them become the primary spiritual influencers in their kids' lives.

Even though I'm a pastor with a vision for kids, I can't lose sight of the even greater vision God has given me as a parent. I'm called to invest in the faith journeys of my three kids, helping them to place their trust firmly in Jesus and learn to live daily for him. I was recently blessed to baptize my eldest daughter, Emma. As part of that event, I also got to hear her testimony of God's work in her life. I still get choked up today thinking about a daddy-daughter date we had at a local park across from our house. As we enjoyed our picnic, this beautiful young lady I'd once held in my arms as a baby was now telling me about her love for God and verbalizing her dreams for the future. I kept asking myself how she got to be so big and where the time had gone. "Didn't she just learn to read? How did she learn so much in such a short time?" I remember the exuberance and passion on her face as she articulated her faith and talked about her excitement to share that faith with her family and friends. I also remember feeling a bit of fear when she said she was wondering if God might be calling her to be a missionary.

As I listened to my daughter, I wondered how God could have possibly used me—a broken vessel—as an instrument to pass the faith on to this maturing young girl. Regardless of my flaws and insecurities, God has blessed me to play a crucial role in her faith journey, and I'm forever thankful for that. It's also a blessing I want every parent to experience as their kids grow in the faith. It's the hope you and I need to have for every parent who comes through the doors of our churches. We all love the idea of being a hero to the kids in our ministries. But an even greater vision is to make every parent in our ministries the spiritual heroes in their kids' lives. Imagine what the faith of a generation would look like if you and I (and countless others) could make that vision a reality.

God can use us to reach the next generation for Christ with the great programs and events we offer. What you and I do makes a difference. But as we discussed earlier on, our time with kids and students is limited compared with the time parents have with their kids. Parents have also been given a unique role that no one else can fill. Consequently, it's essential that we see the big picture of equipping parents to be the primary ones

TEAM UP!

shaping their children's faith. It's not that we have to stop providing incredible programs and environments; it's more that we need to weave partnering with parents into the fabric of what we do. For decades we've been painting incomplete pictures by only focusing our attention on kids. It's time to complete those pictures and increase the effect of our ministries by taking greater steps to equip parents to reach the next generation for Christ.

Fast forward 10 or 15 years from now. Think about a couple of the children or students in your ministry. Consider what their faith and lives would look like if their parents were better equipped to invest in their faith journeys. Imagine sitting down with their parents to hear all that God has done and is doing in their children's lives. Envision the tears of joy and excitement as they thank you for your support and constant encouragement. Can you see it? That's the better future you can look forward to as you partner with parents.

We need to reach and equip the next generation for Christ. Deuteronomy 6:4-9 gives us a blueprint for making that happen. Judges 2:10 shows us what's at stake if we don't. And being effective at it takes you, me, and the rest of the faith community committing to partner with parents as they pass their faith on to their kids.

Let the journey begin today. It's time to team up!